I0446965

# SUMPTUOUS *coloring book* LANDSCAPES

ISBN 9798870331539

**Editor**

*Benoit Portier*
*77 chemin de la curiaz*
*73230 Saint-Alban-Leysse, France*

Legal Deposit Nov. 2023
Printed on demand by Amazon

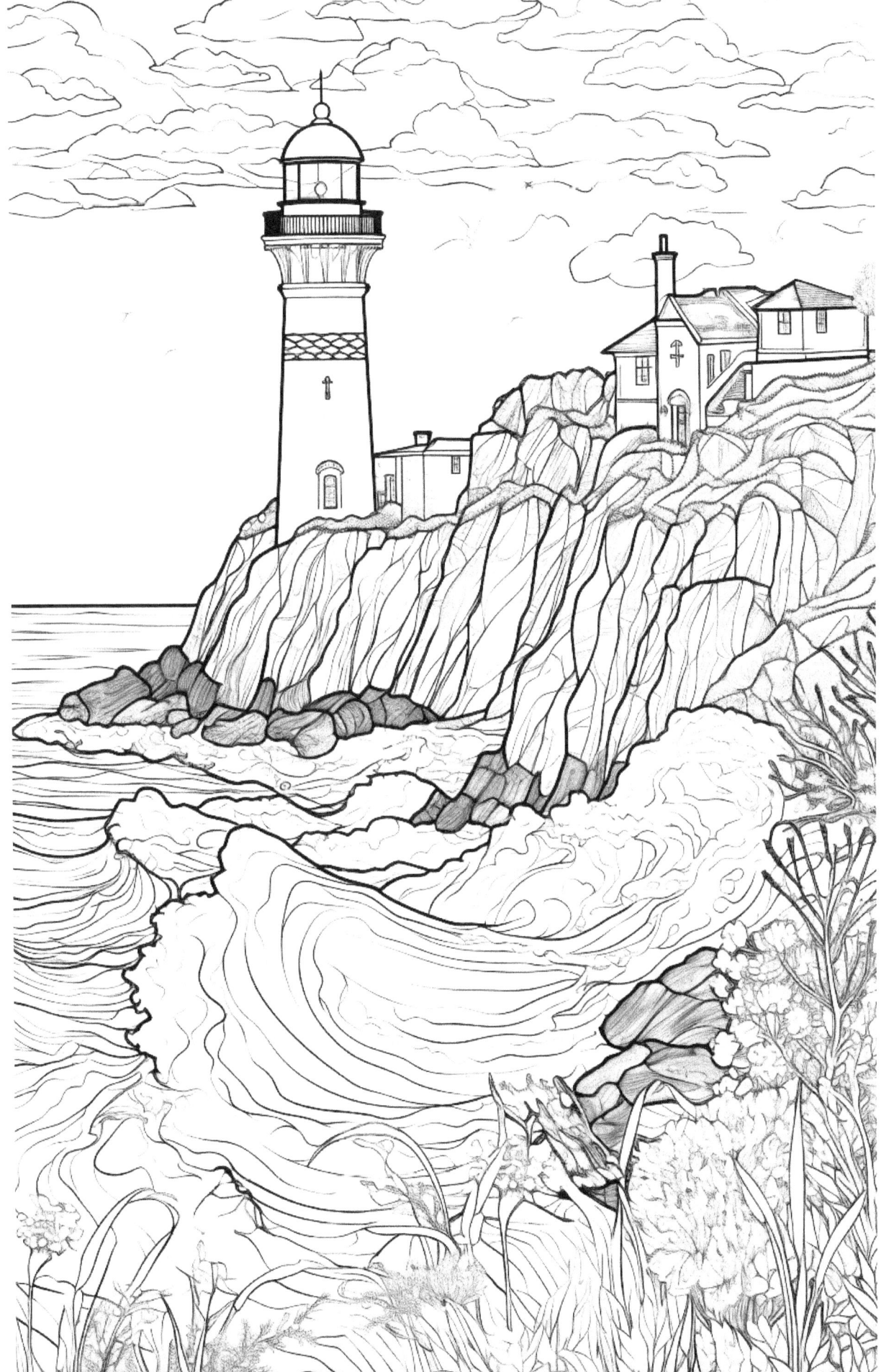

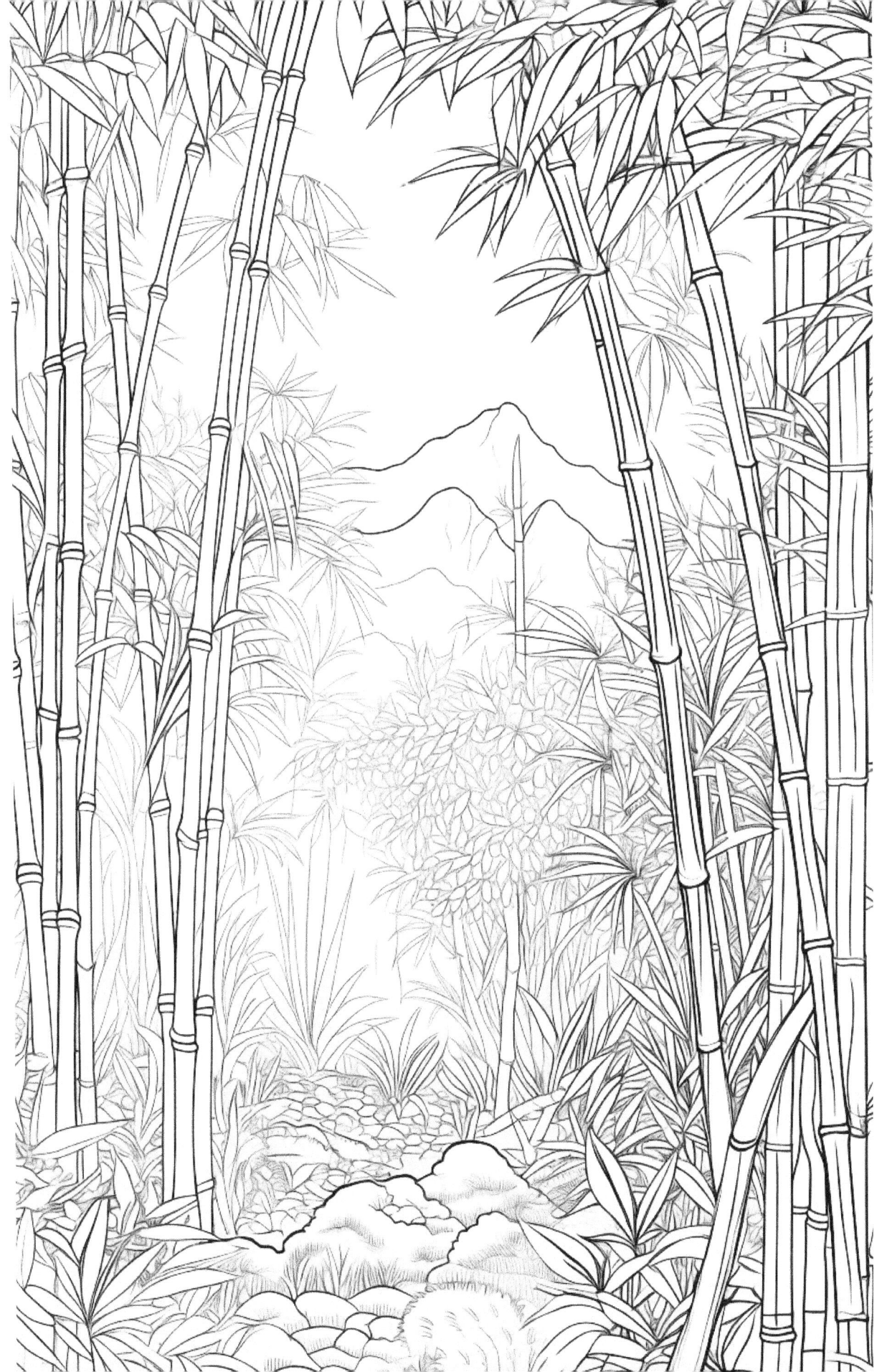

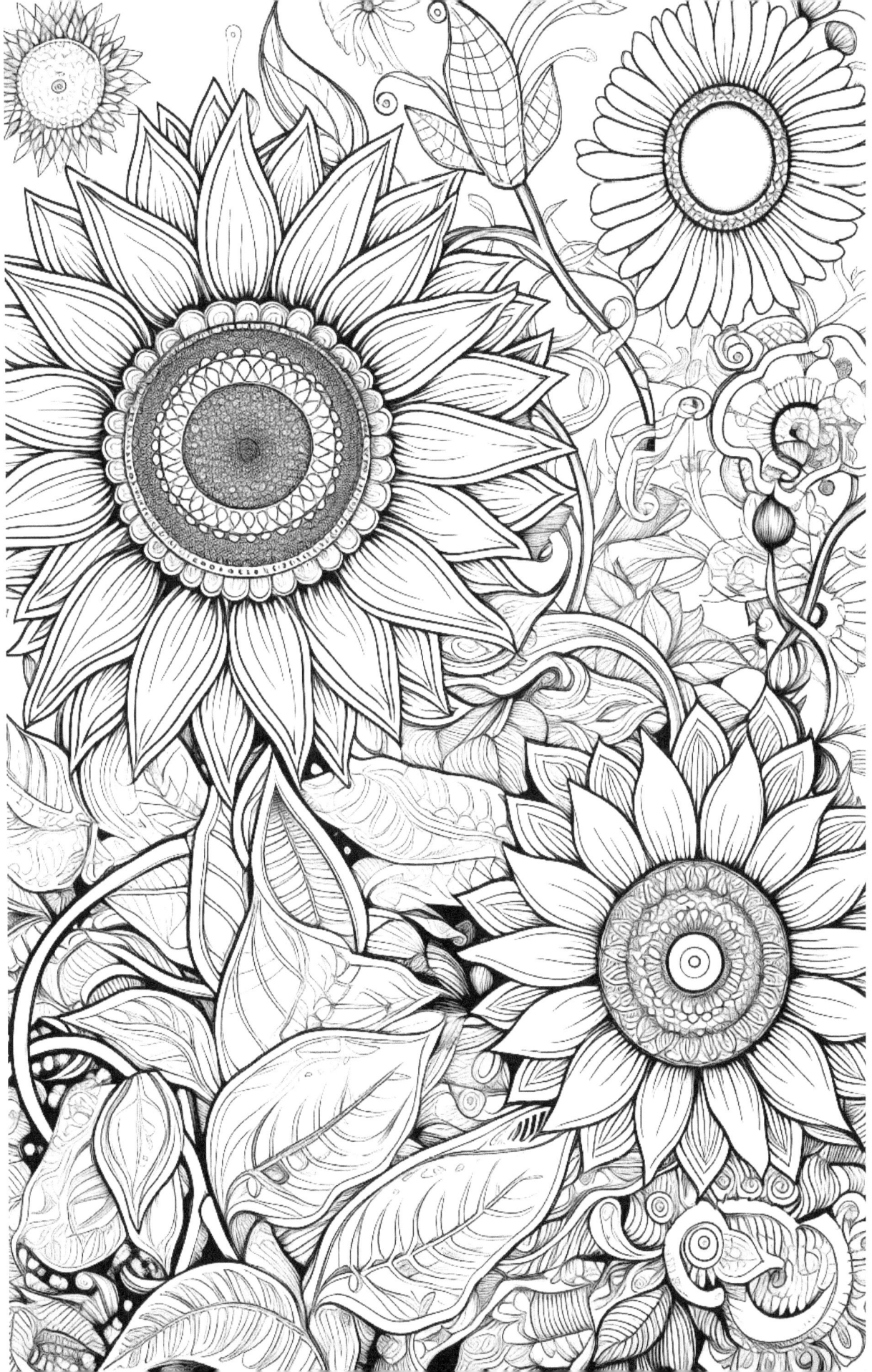

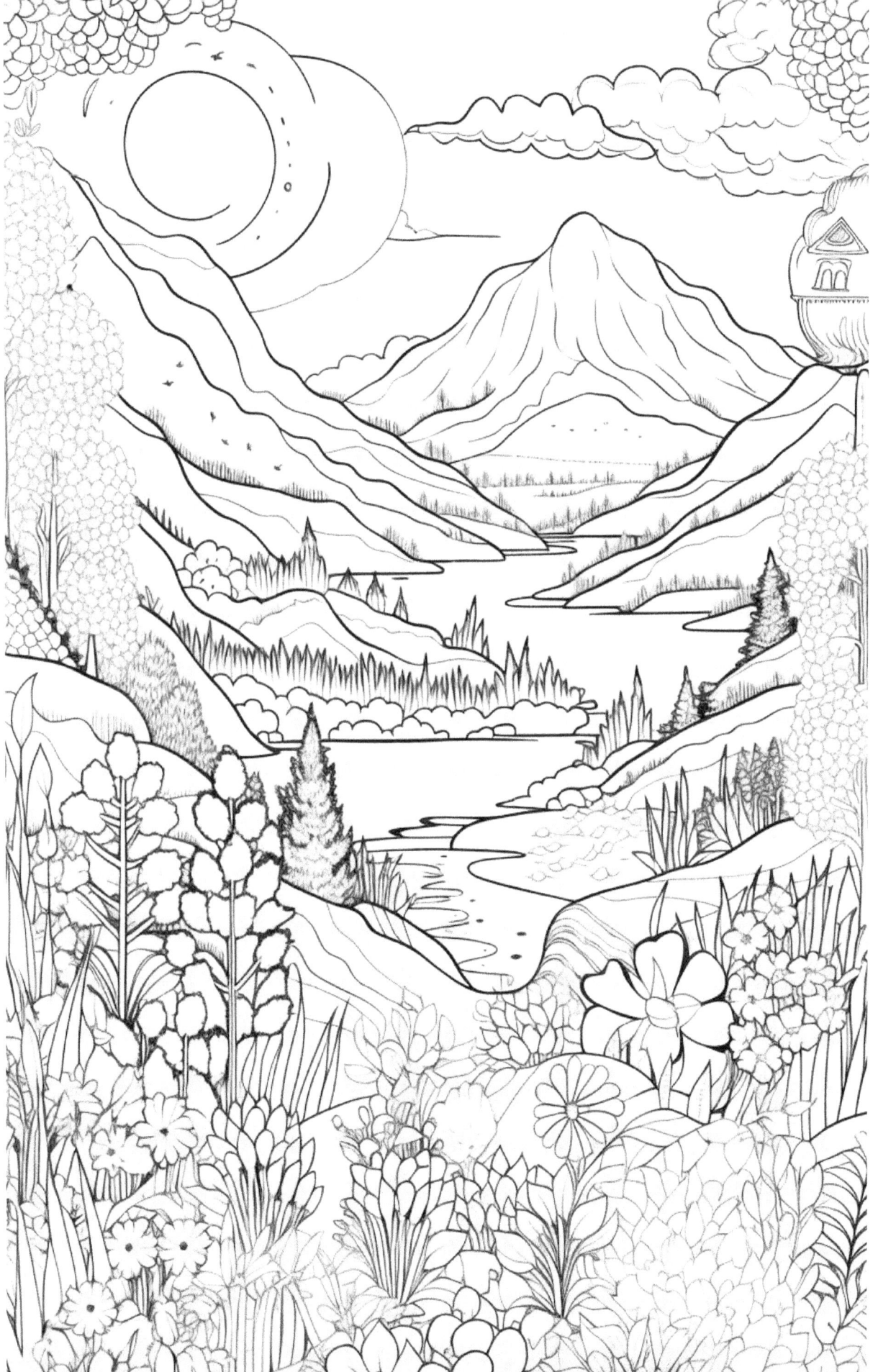

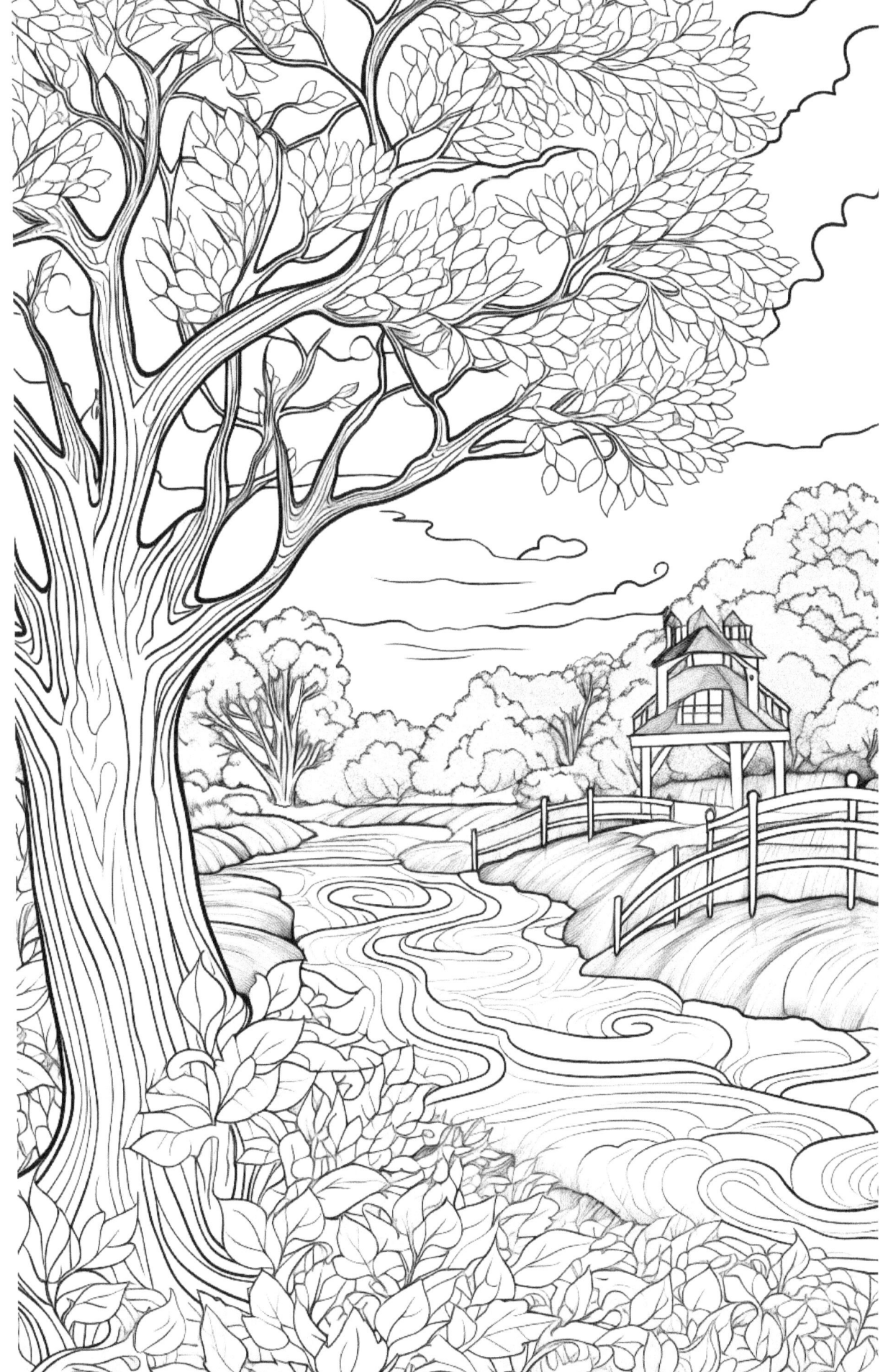

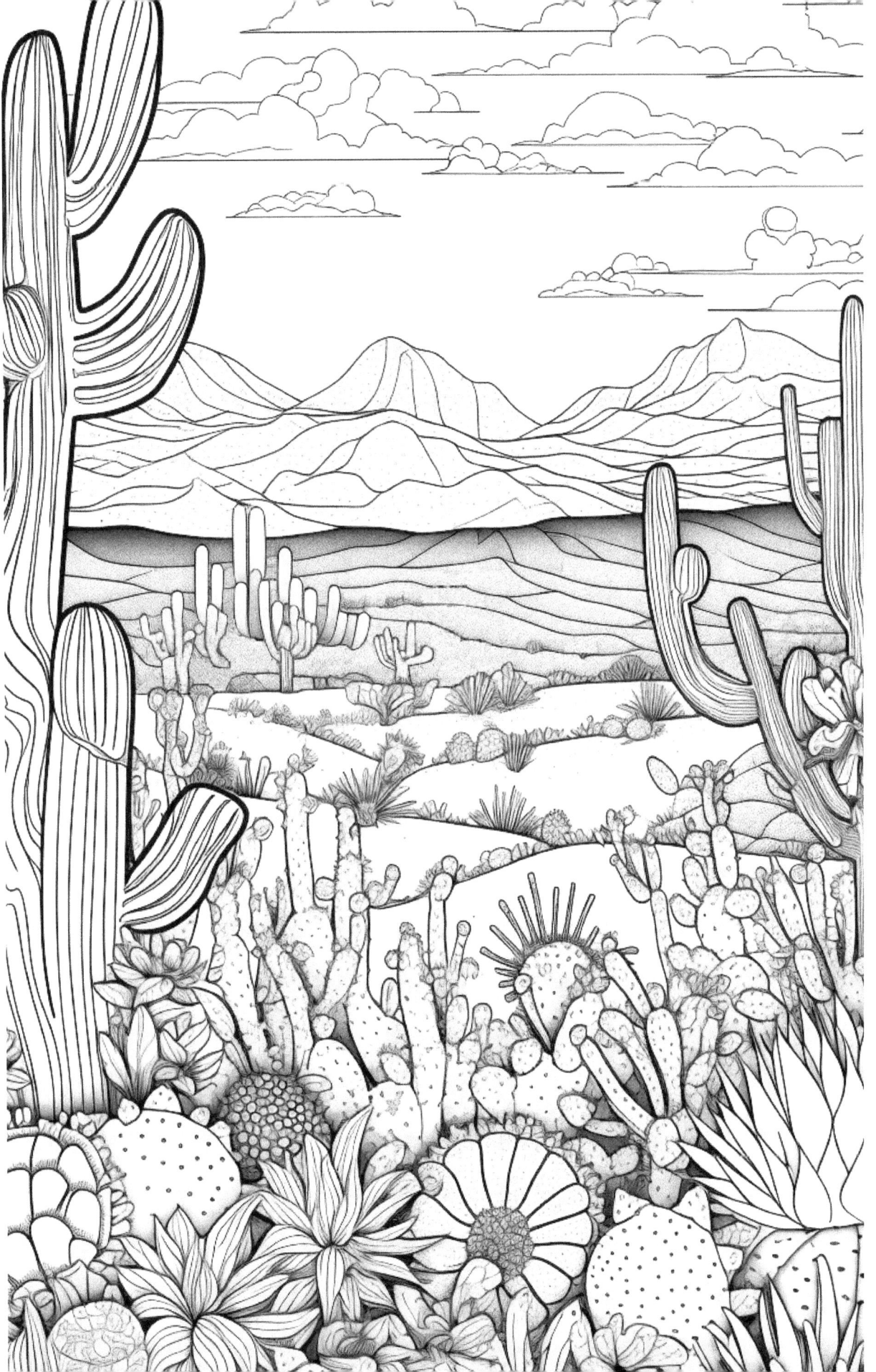

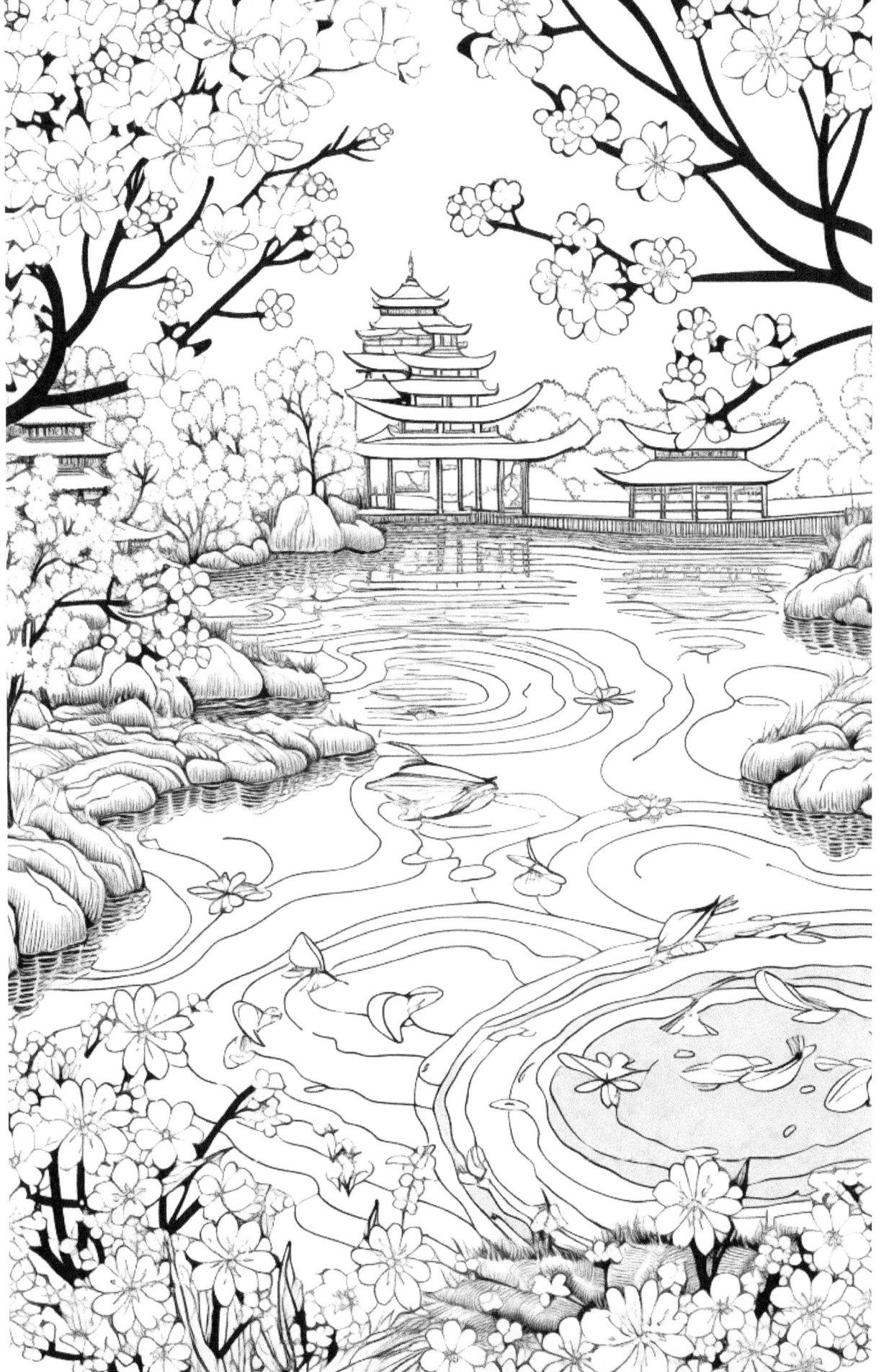

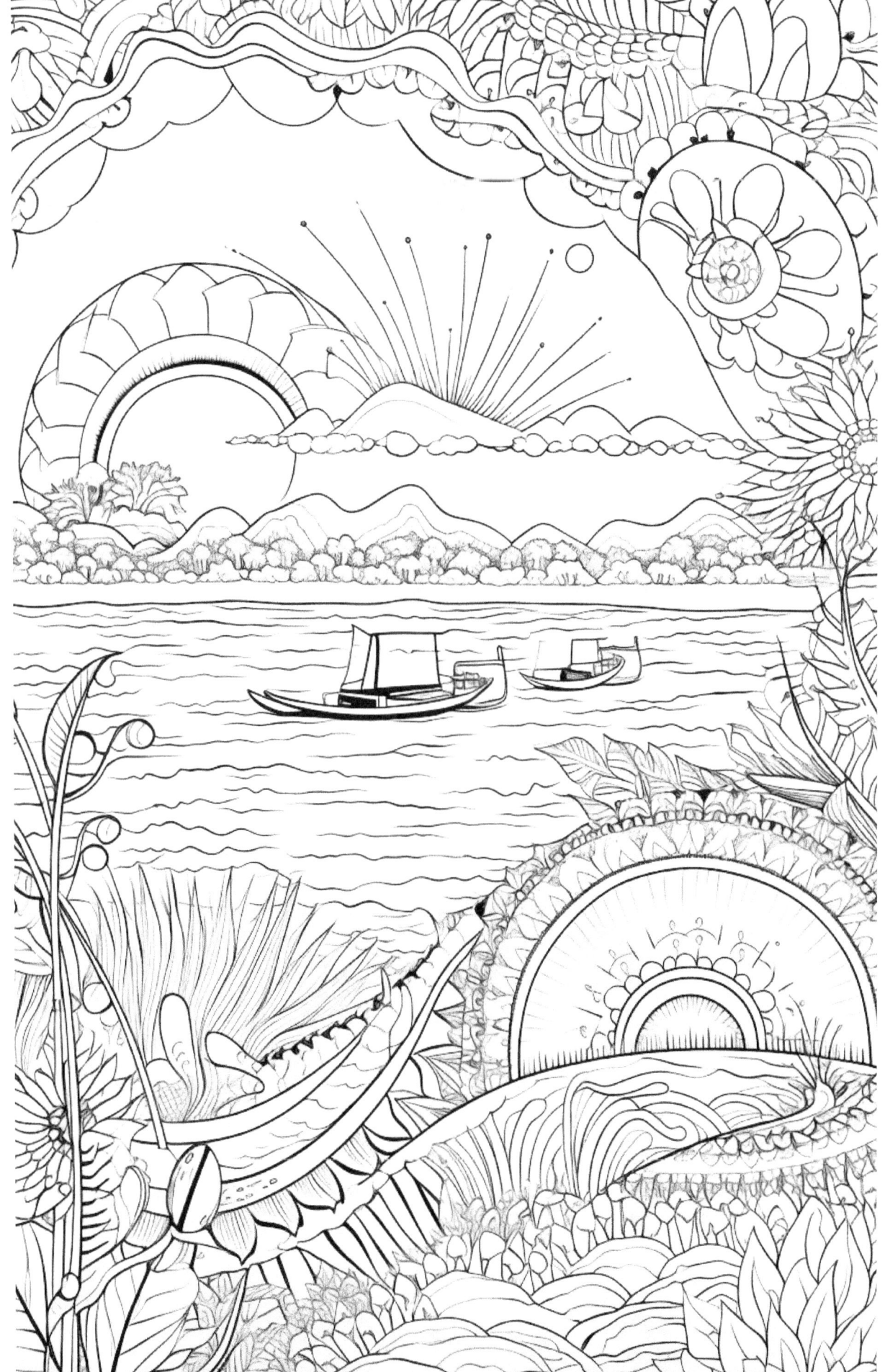

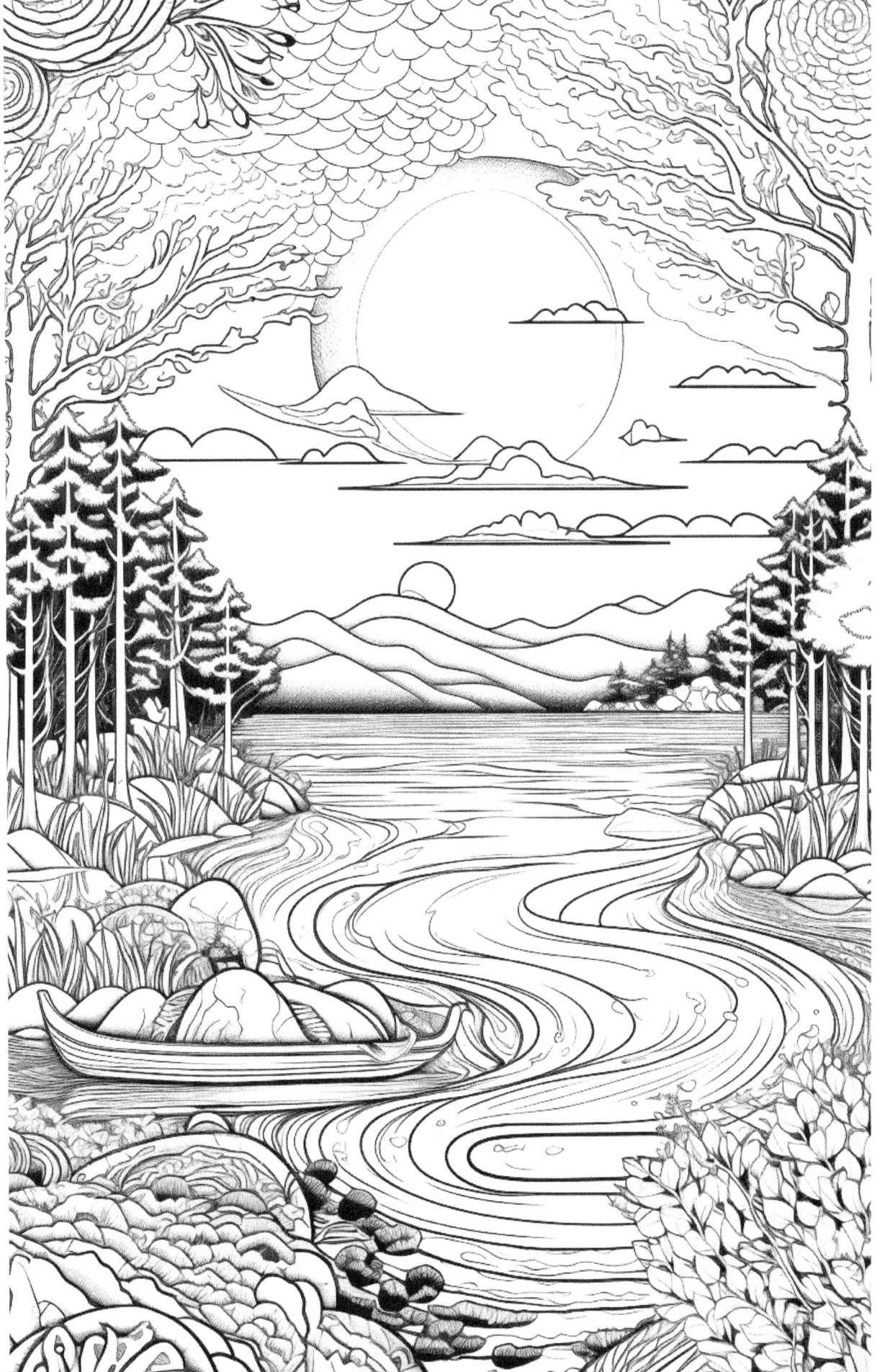

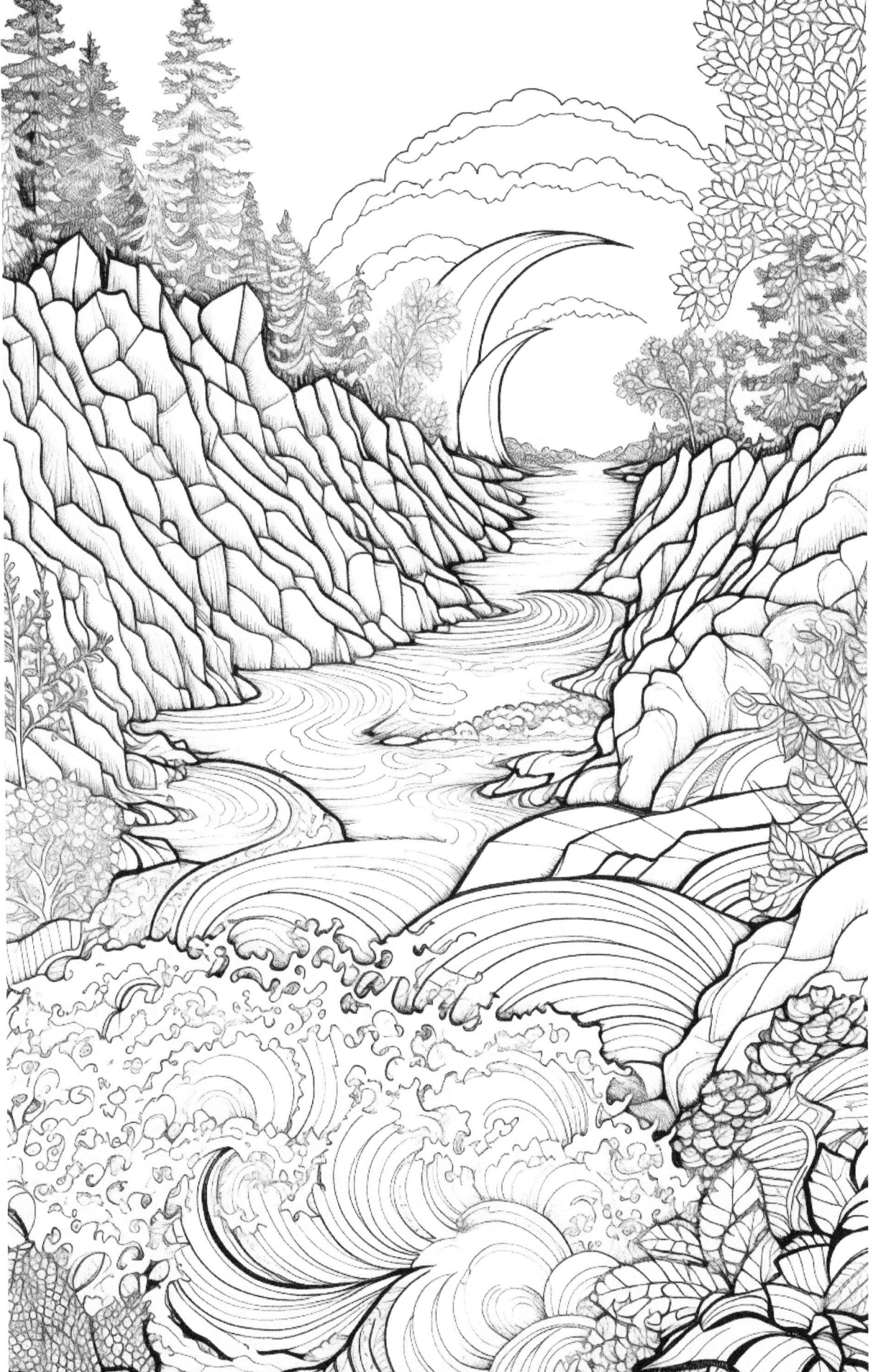

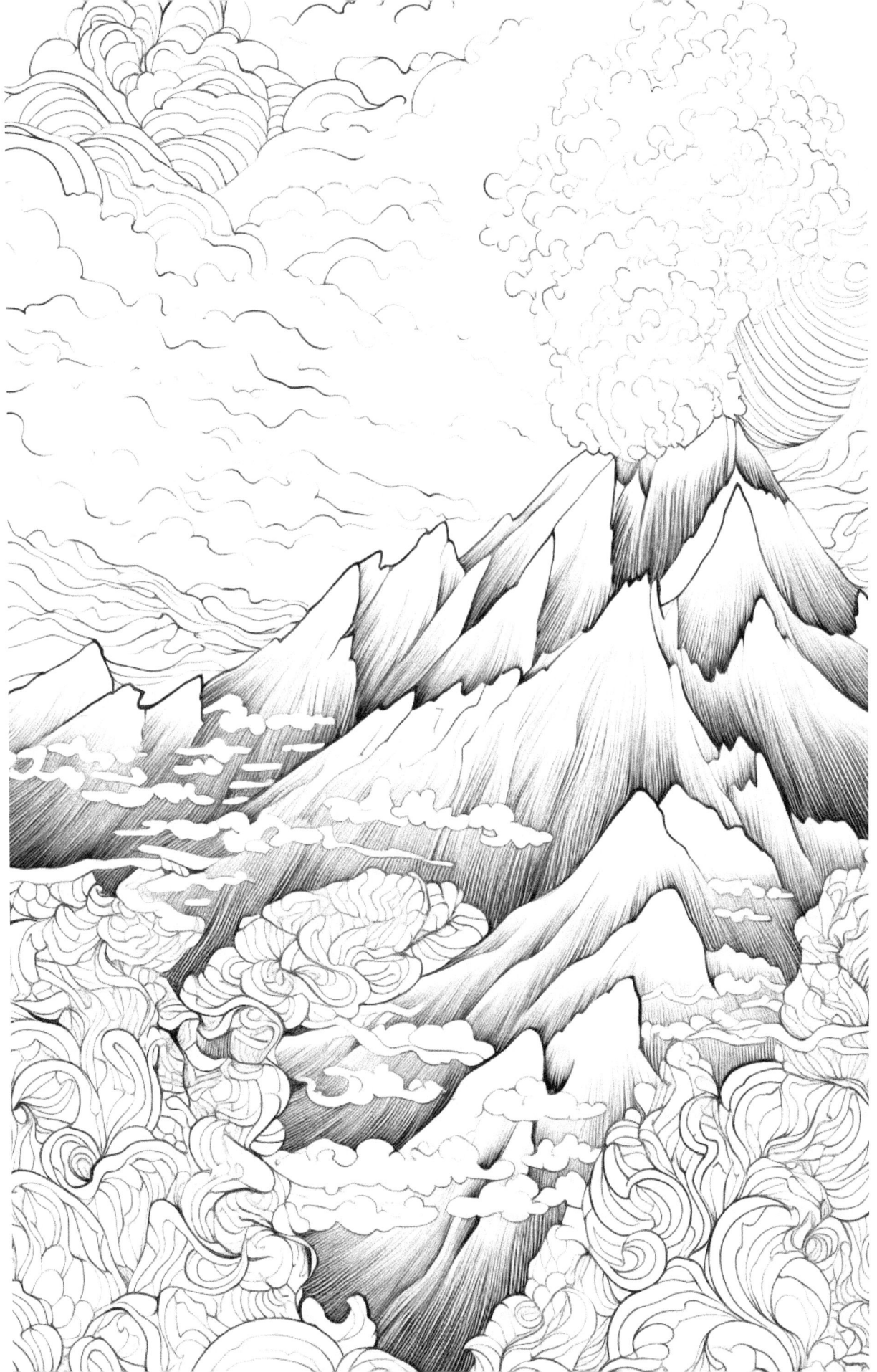

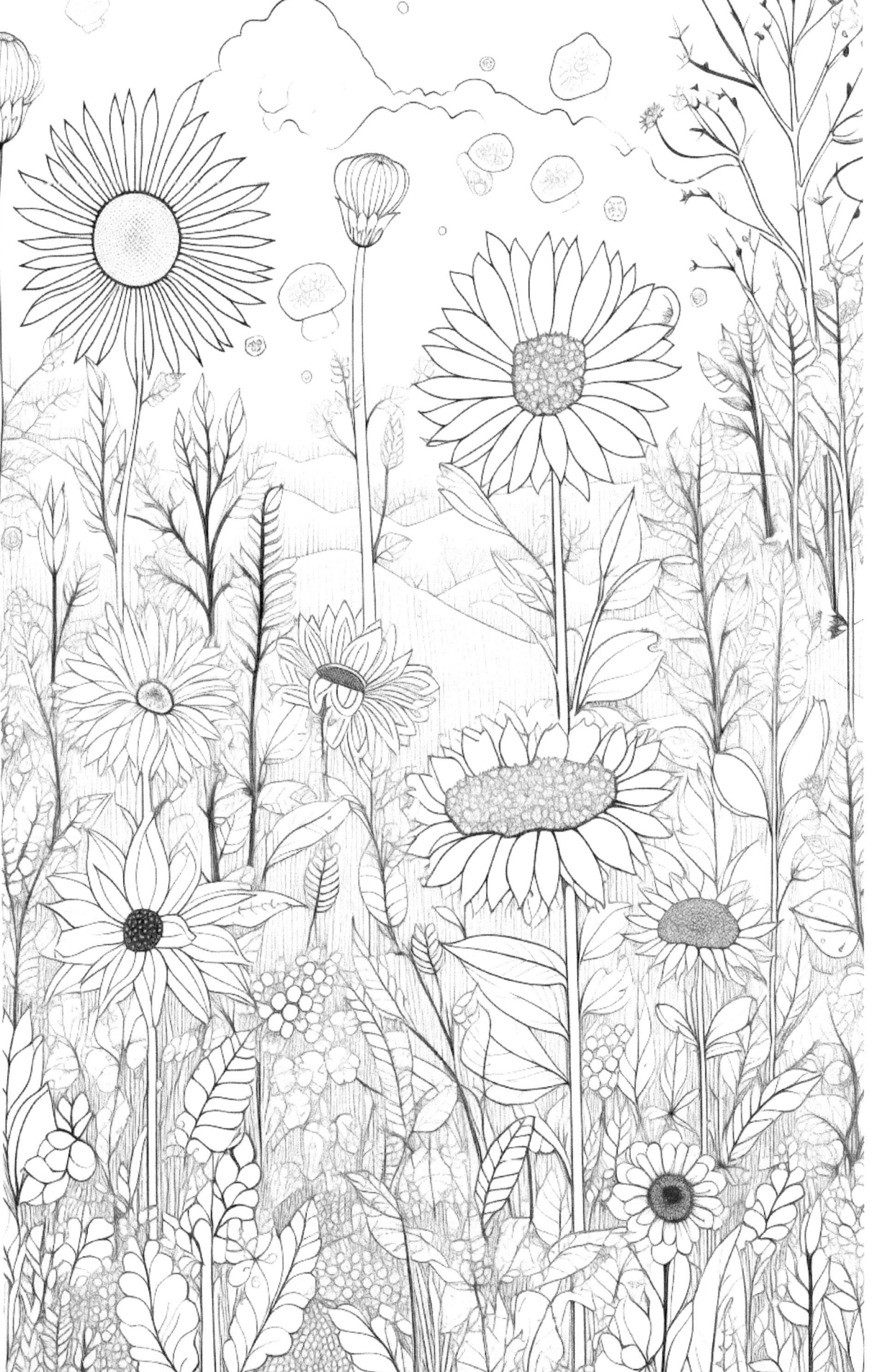

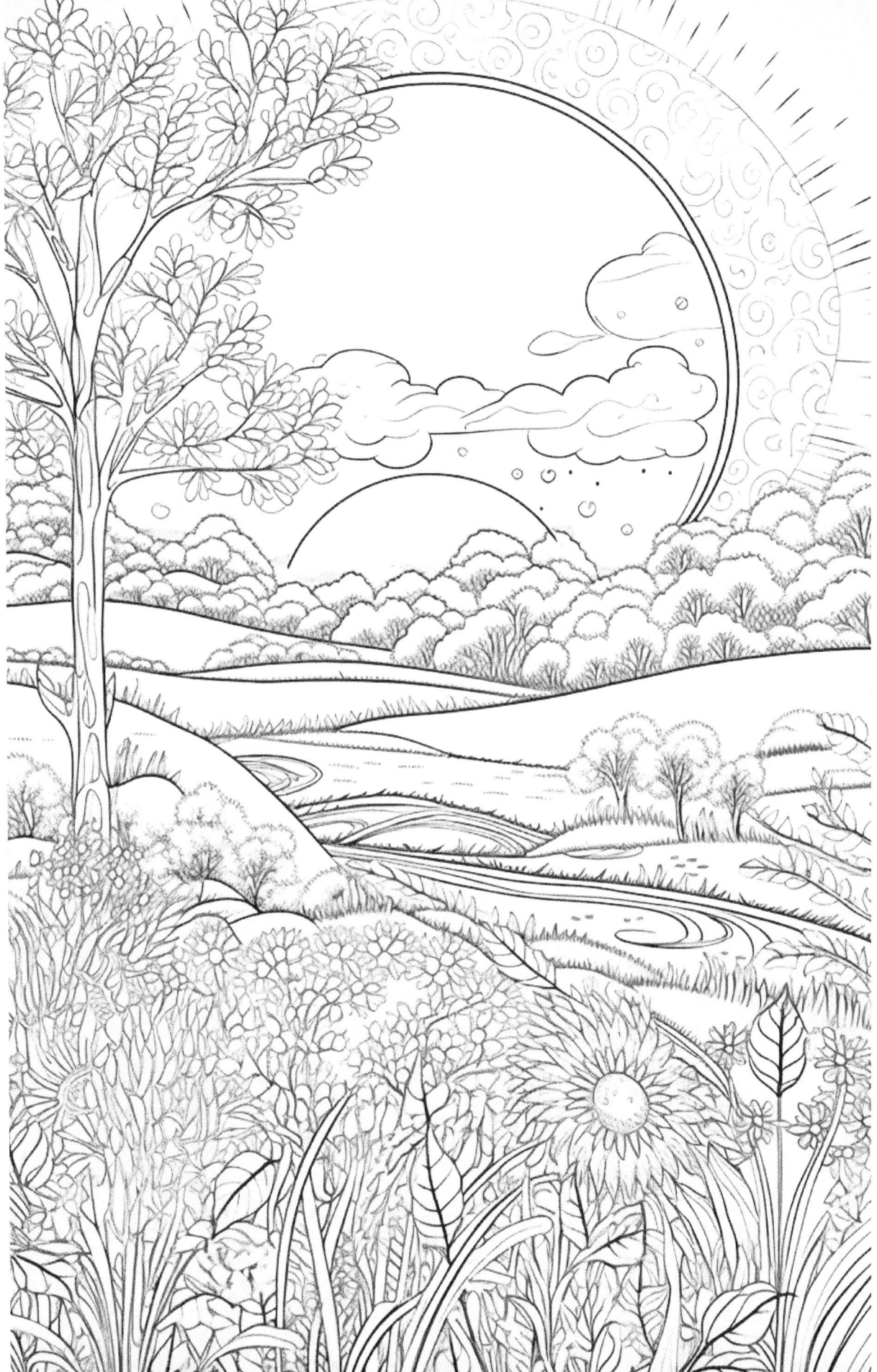

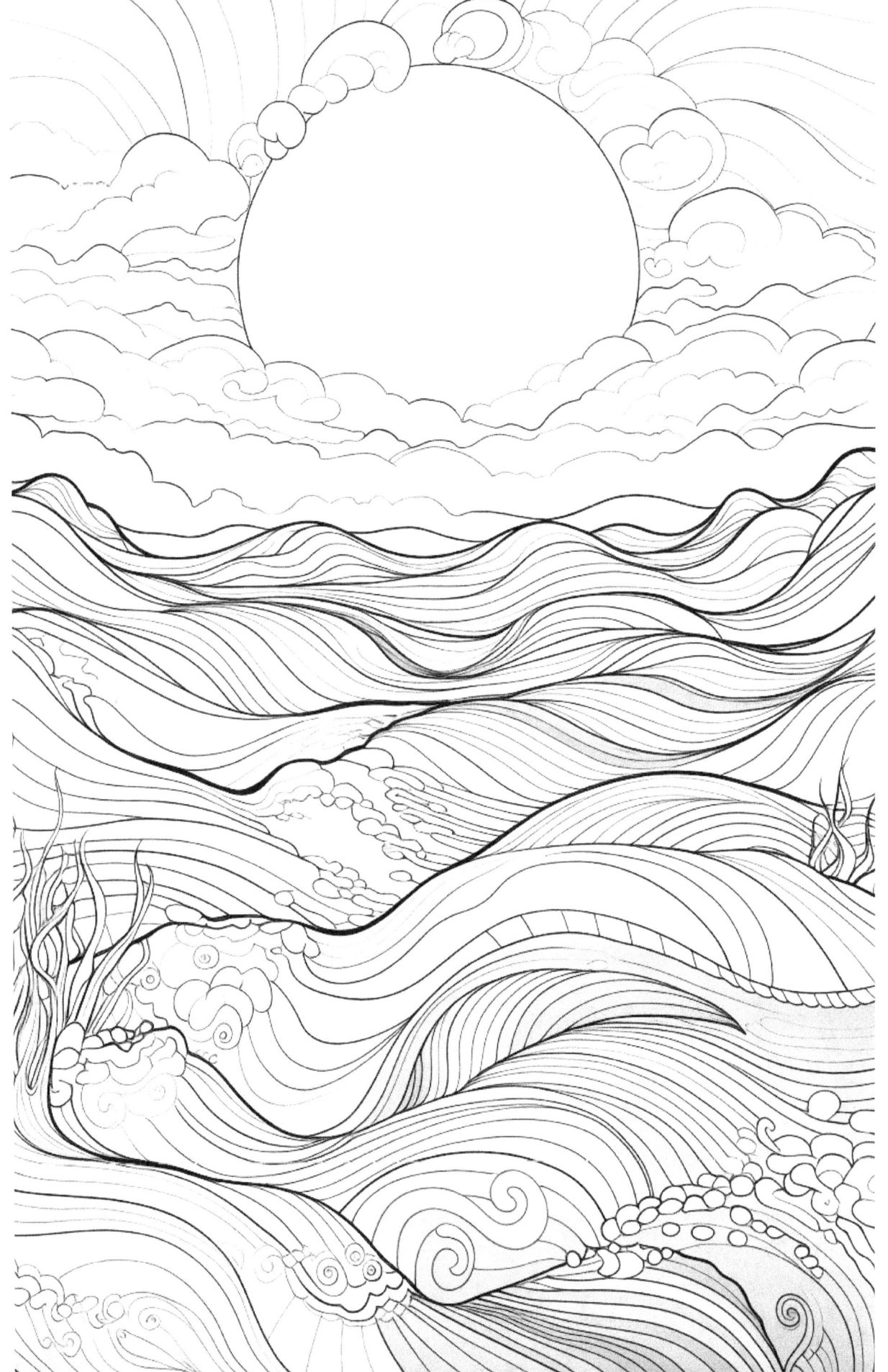

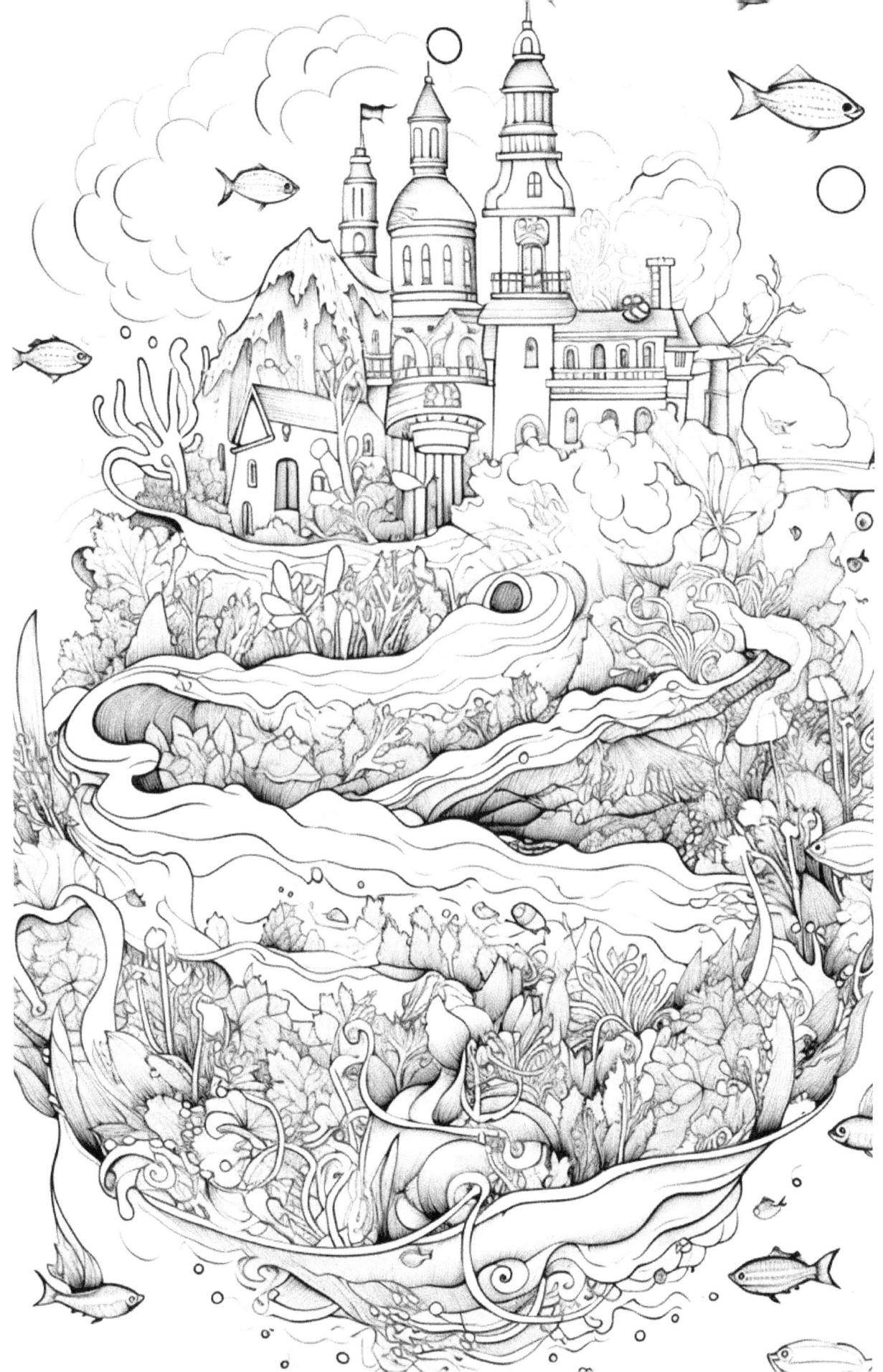

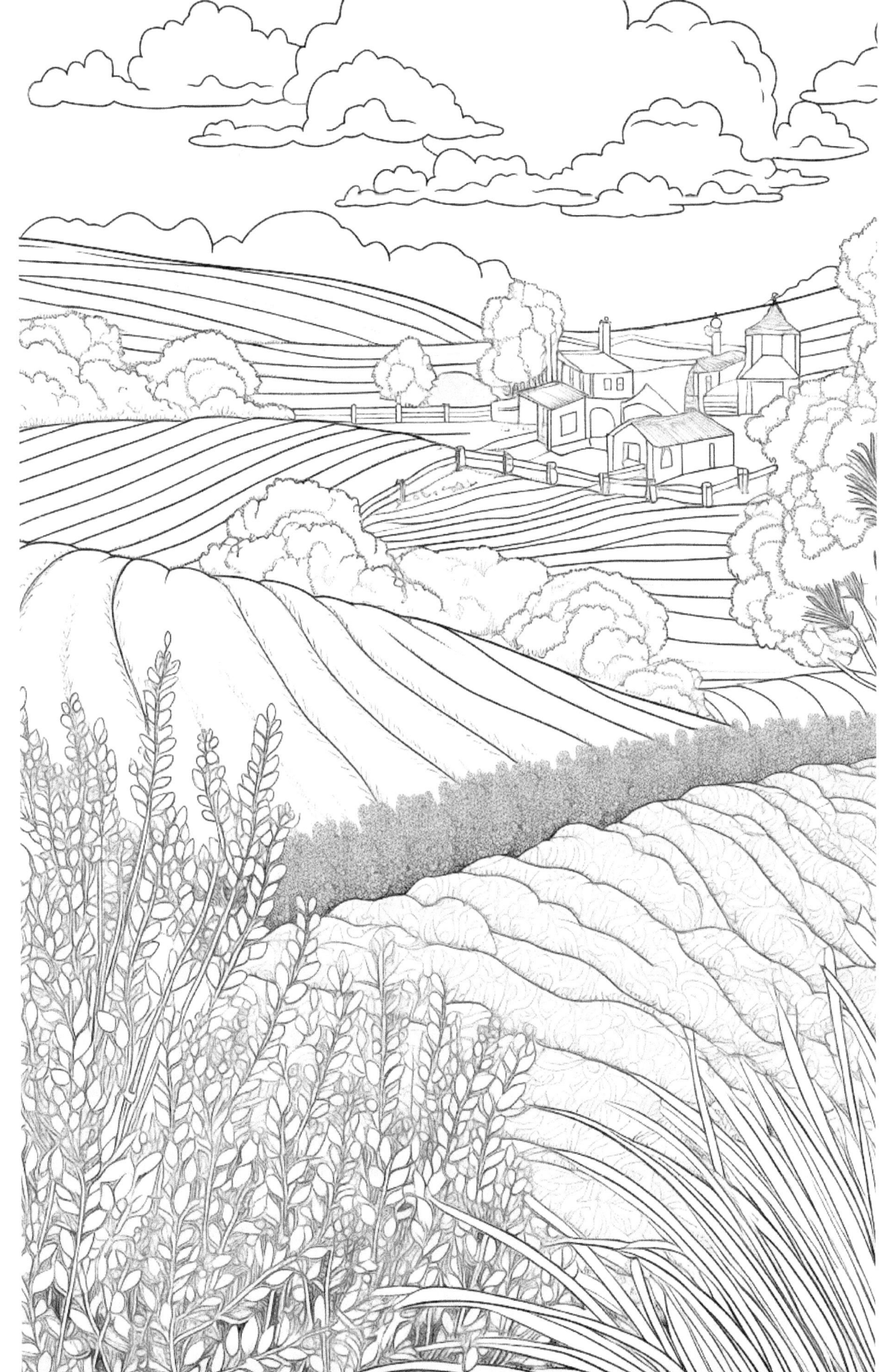

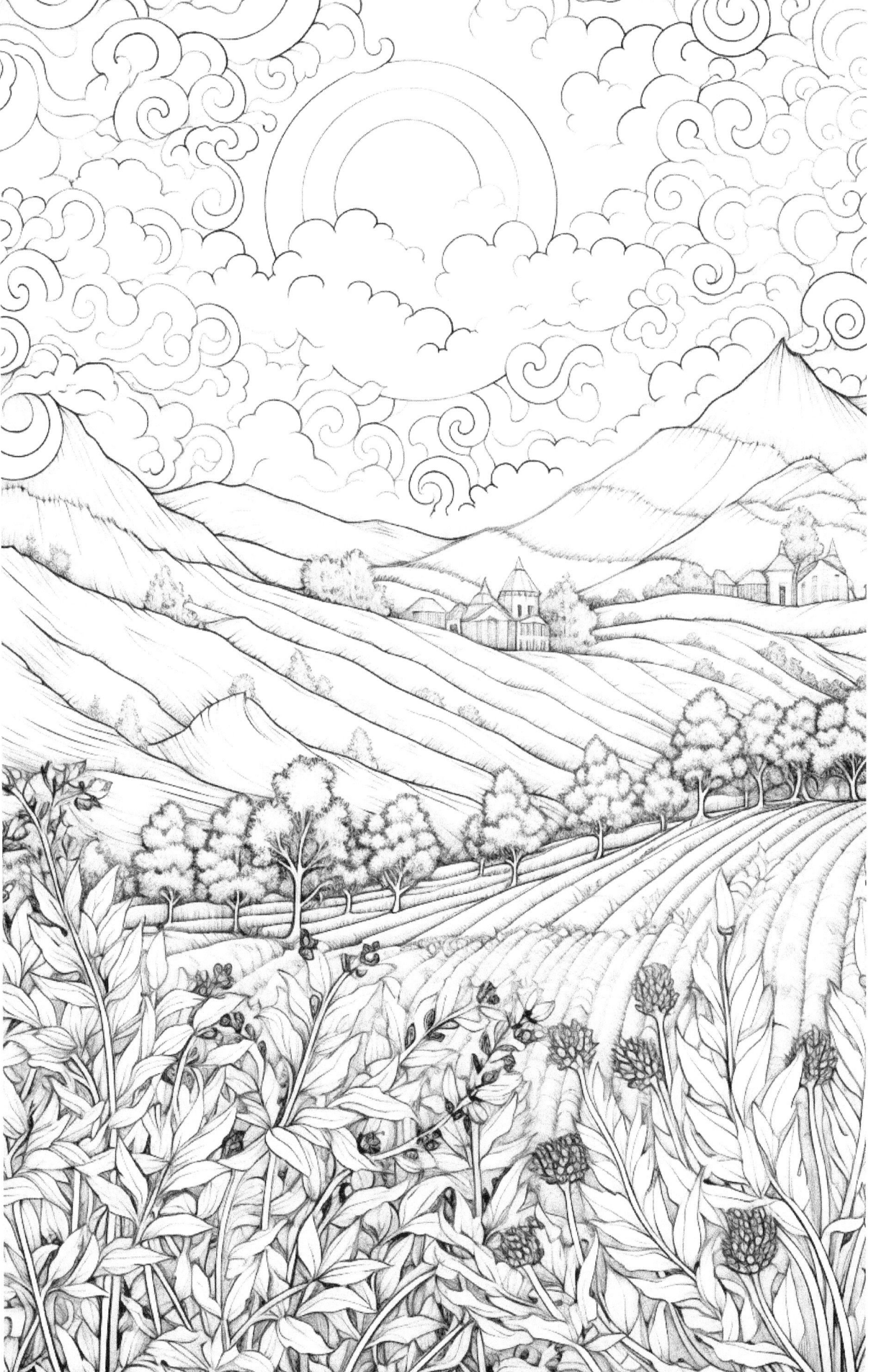

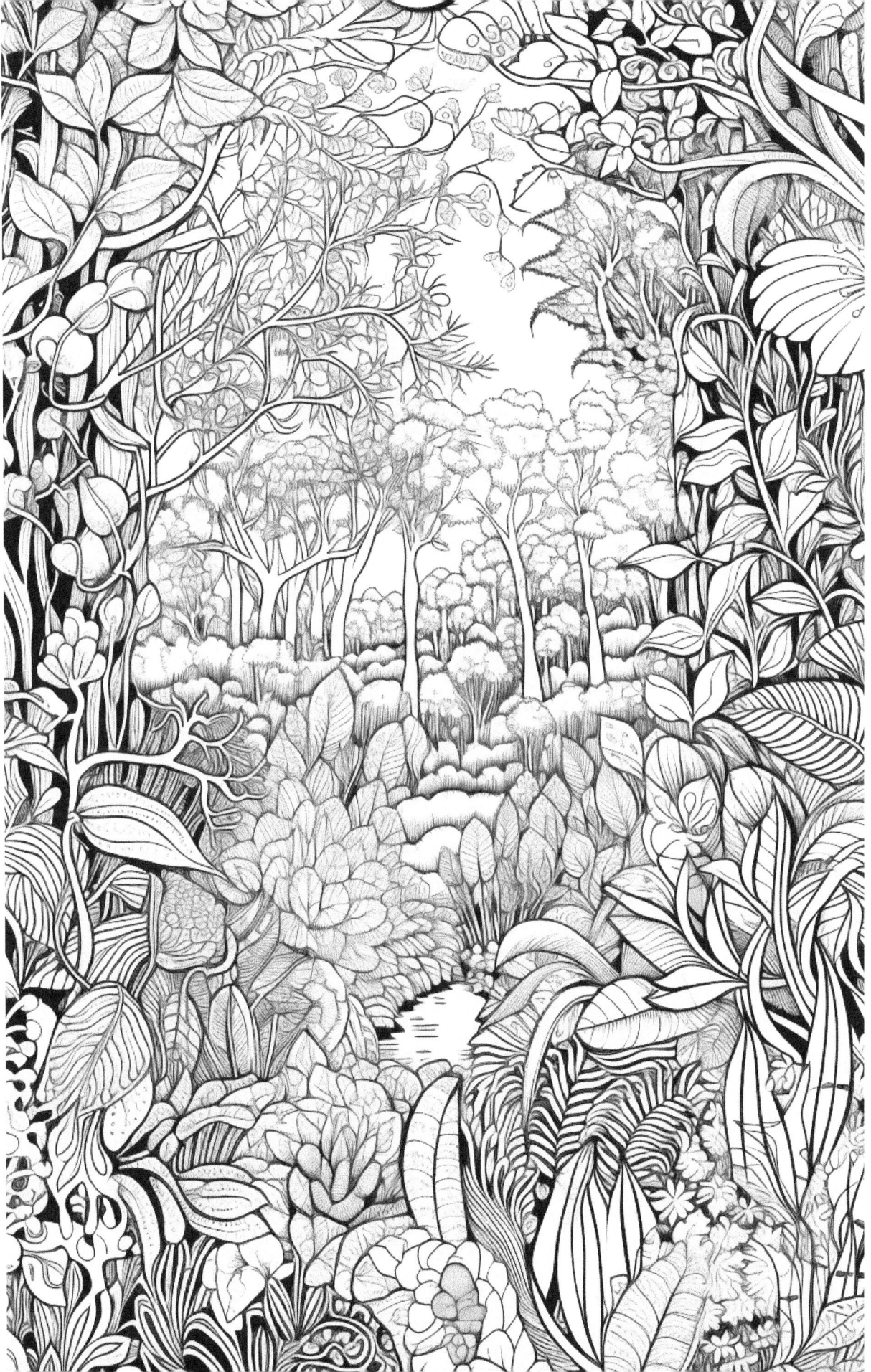

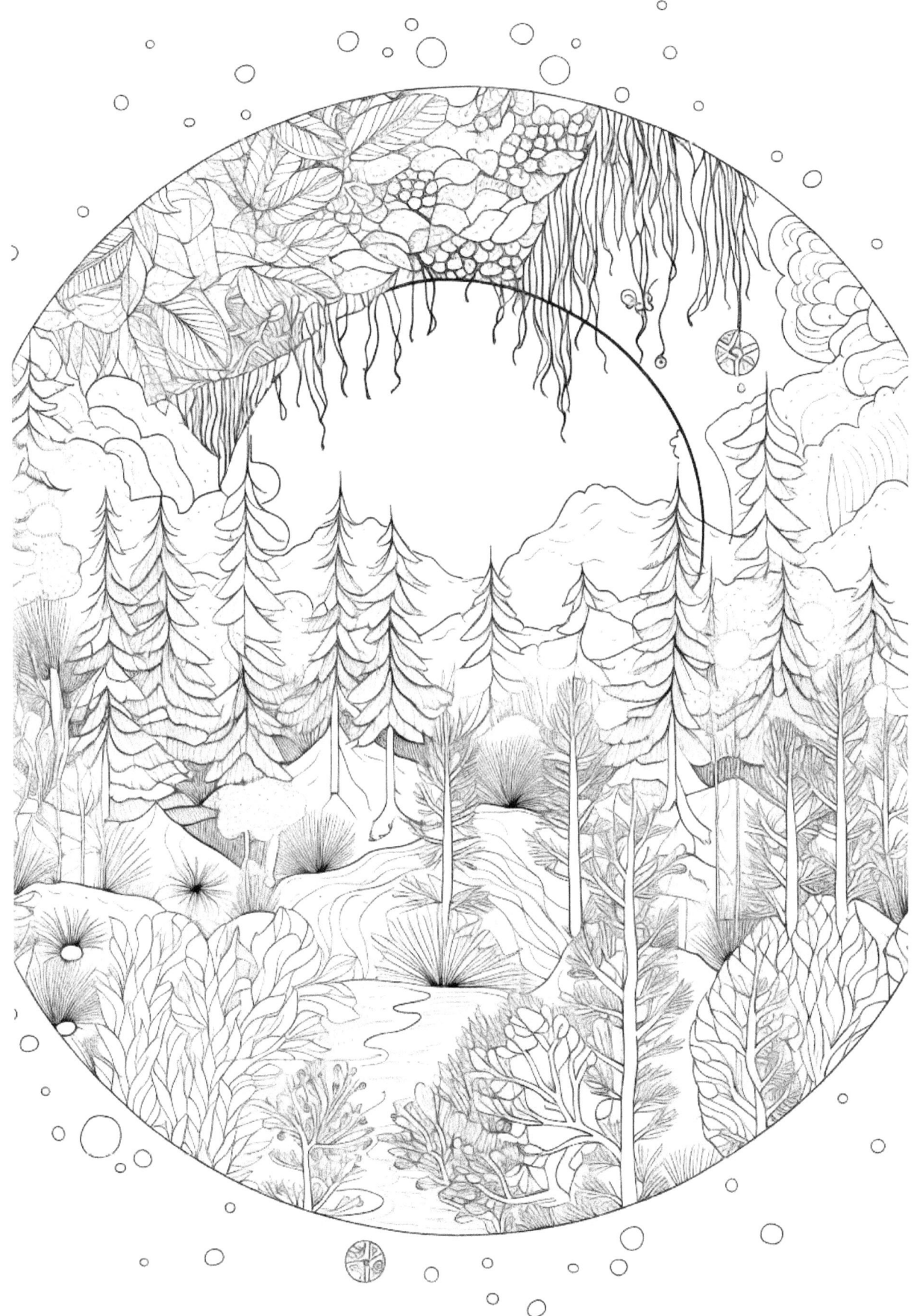

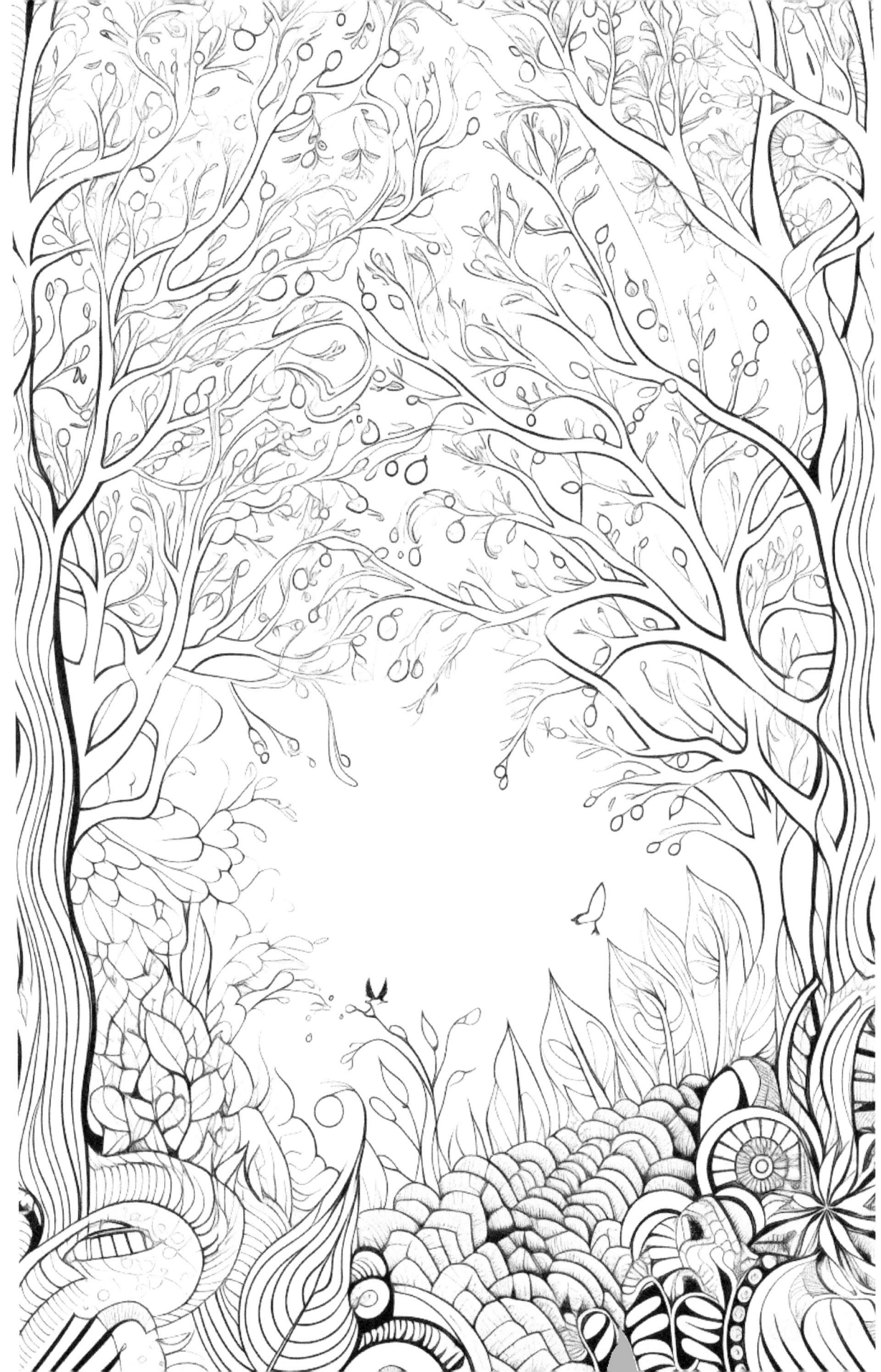

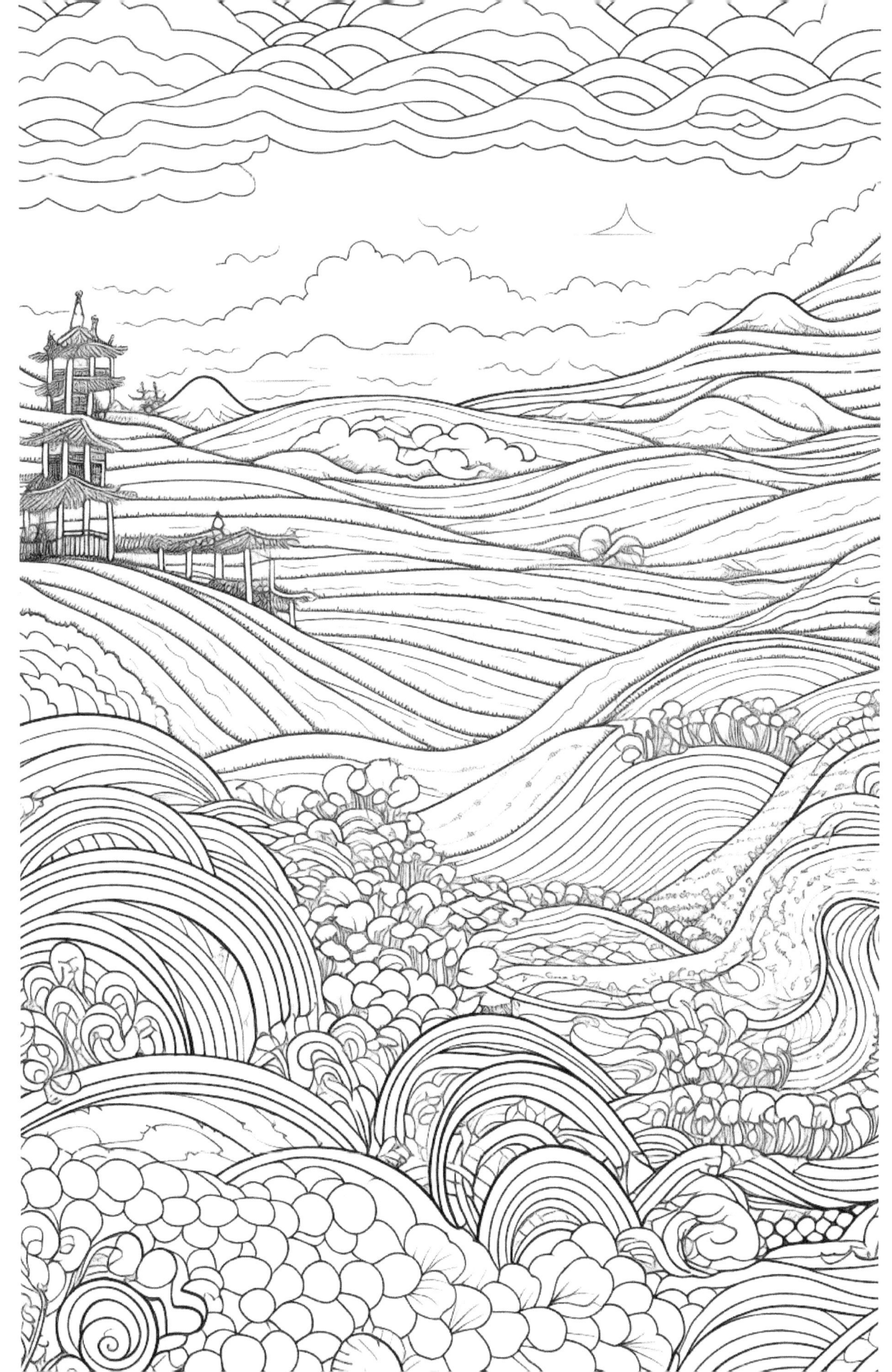

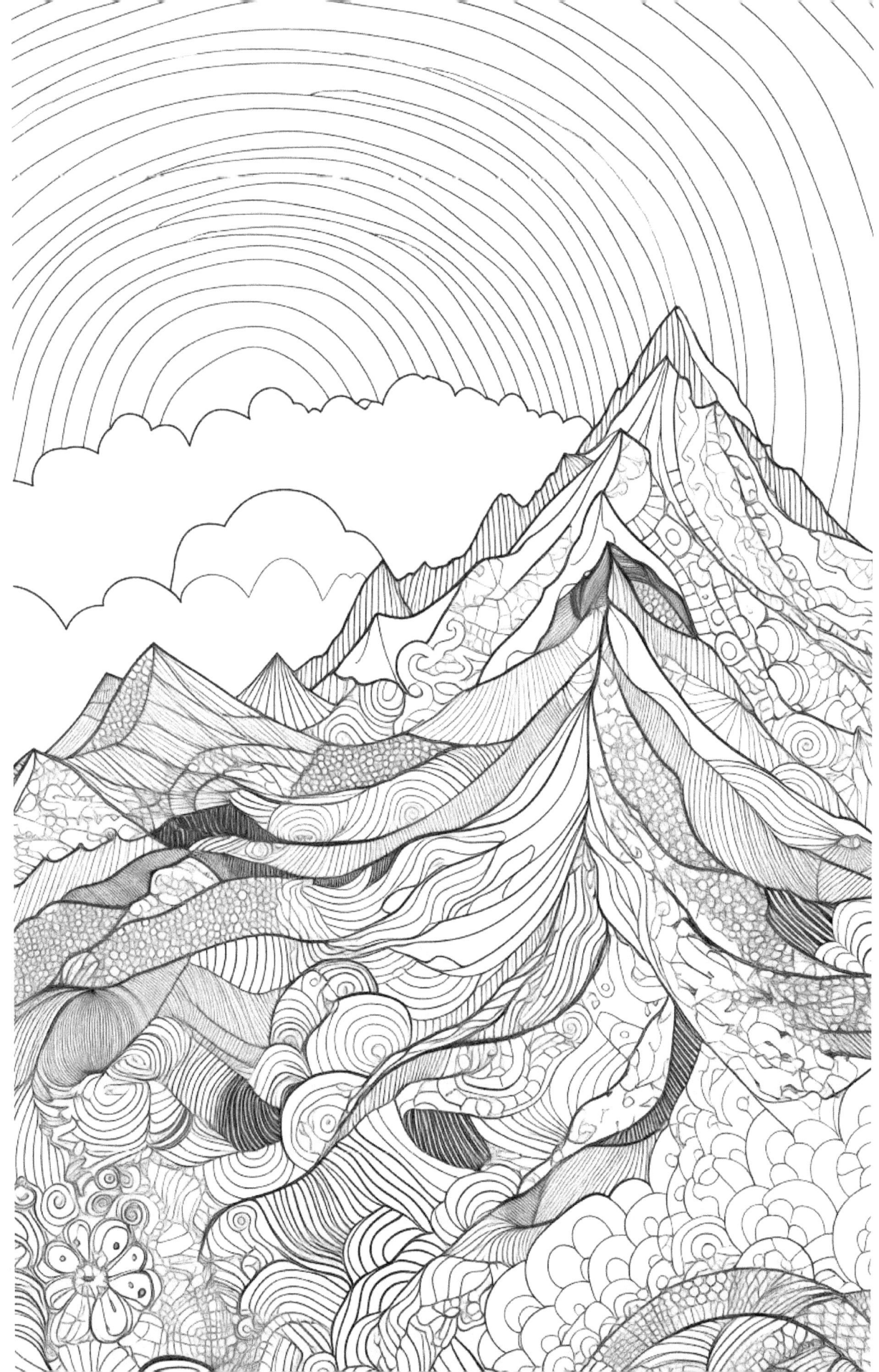

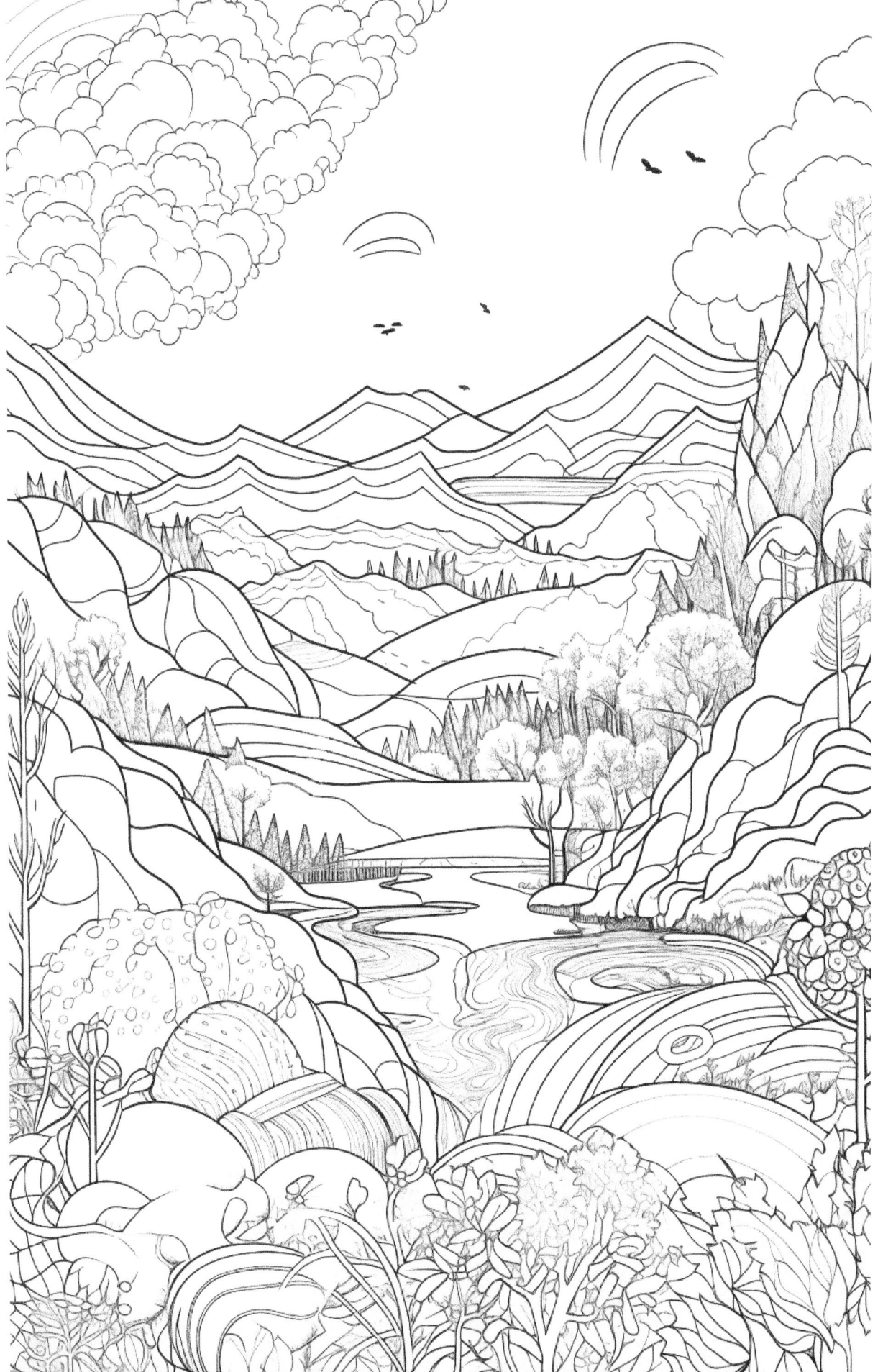

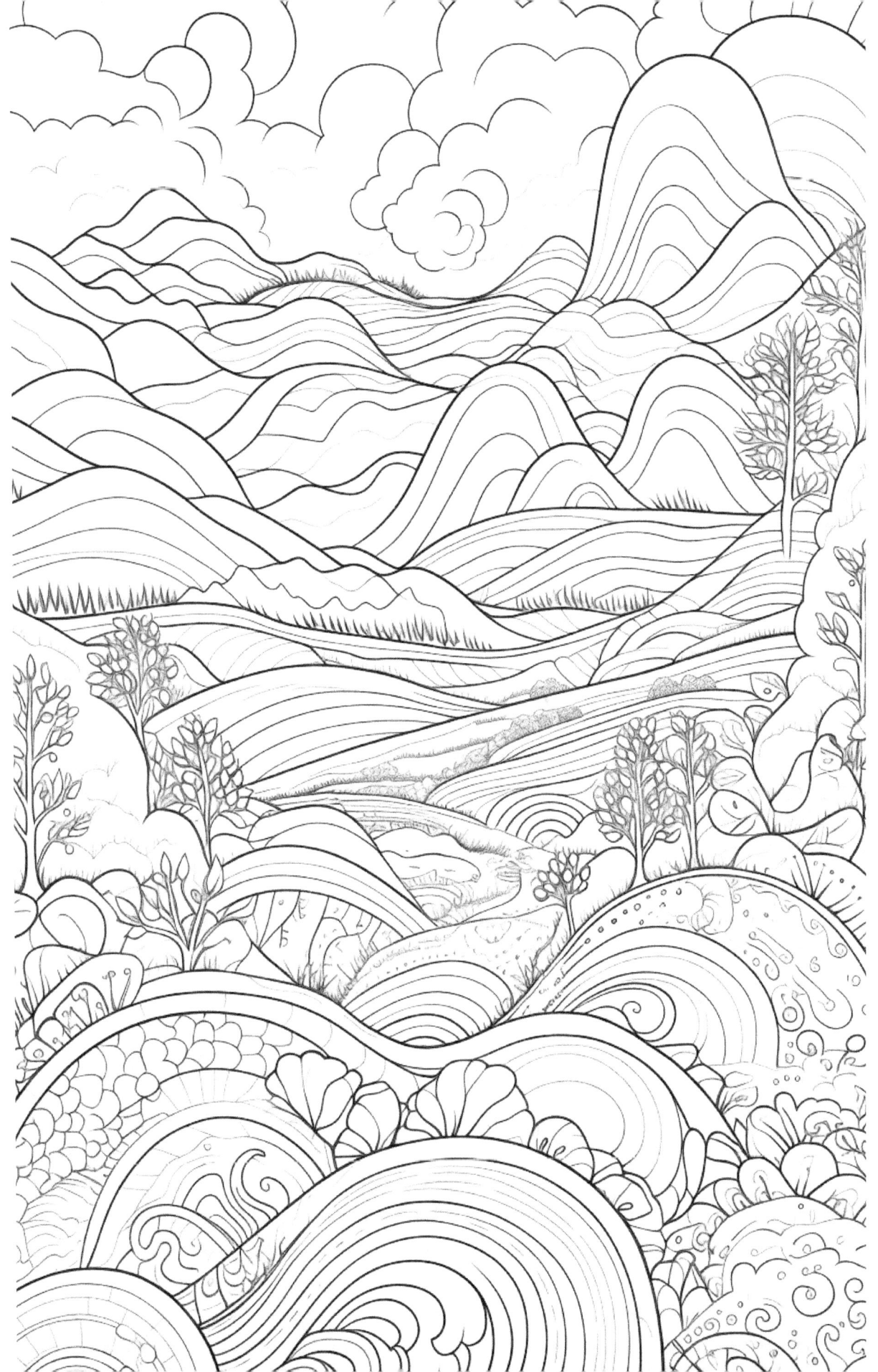

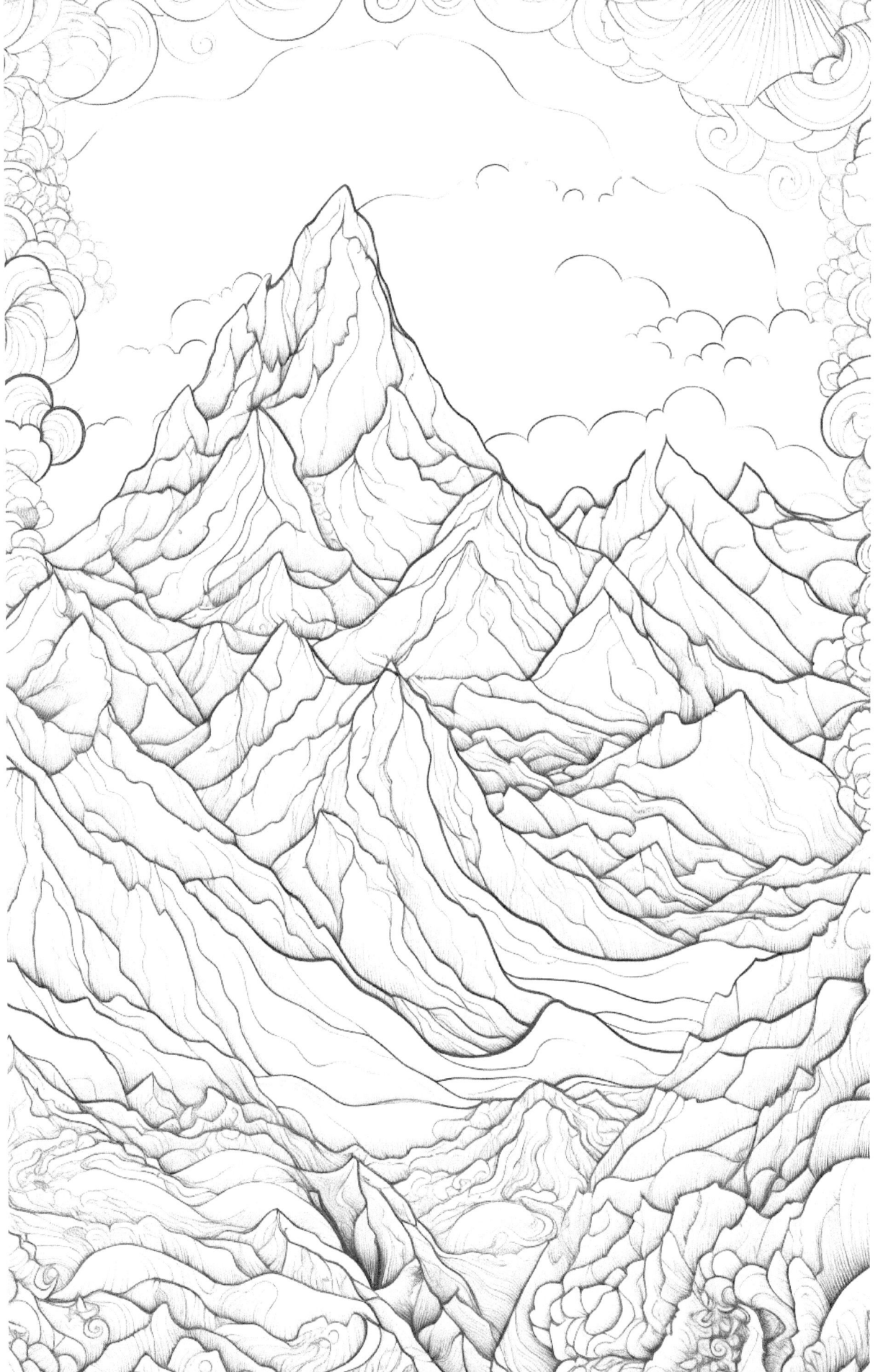

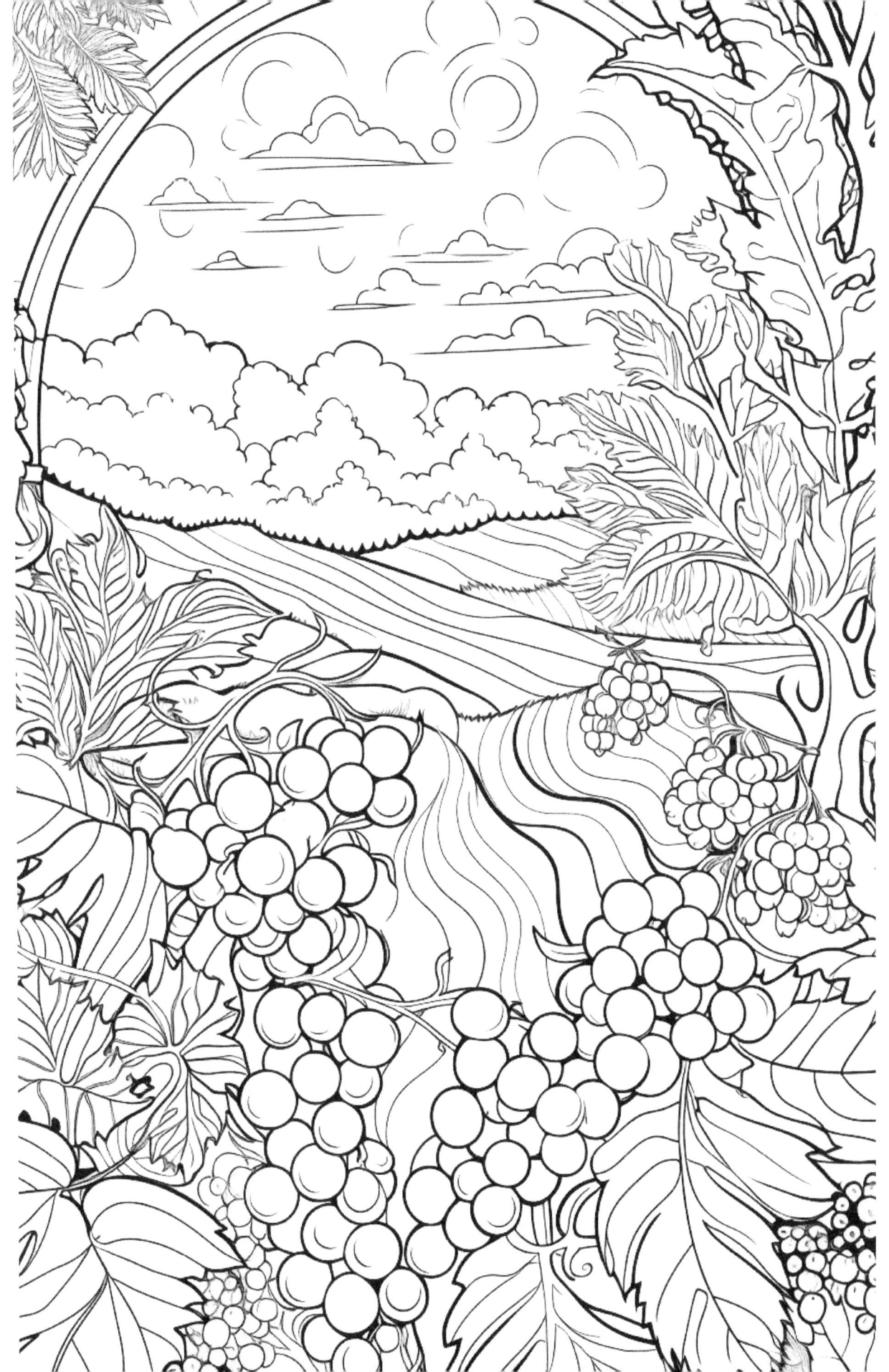

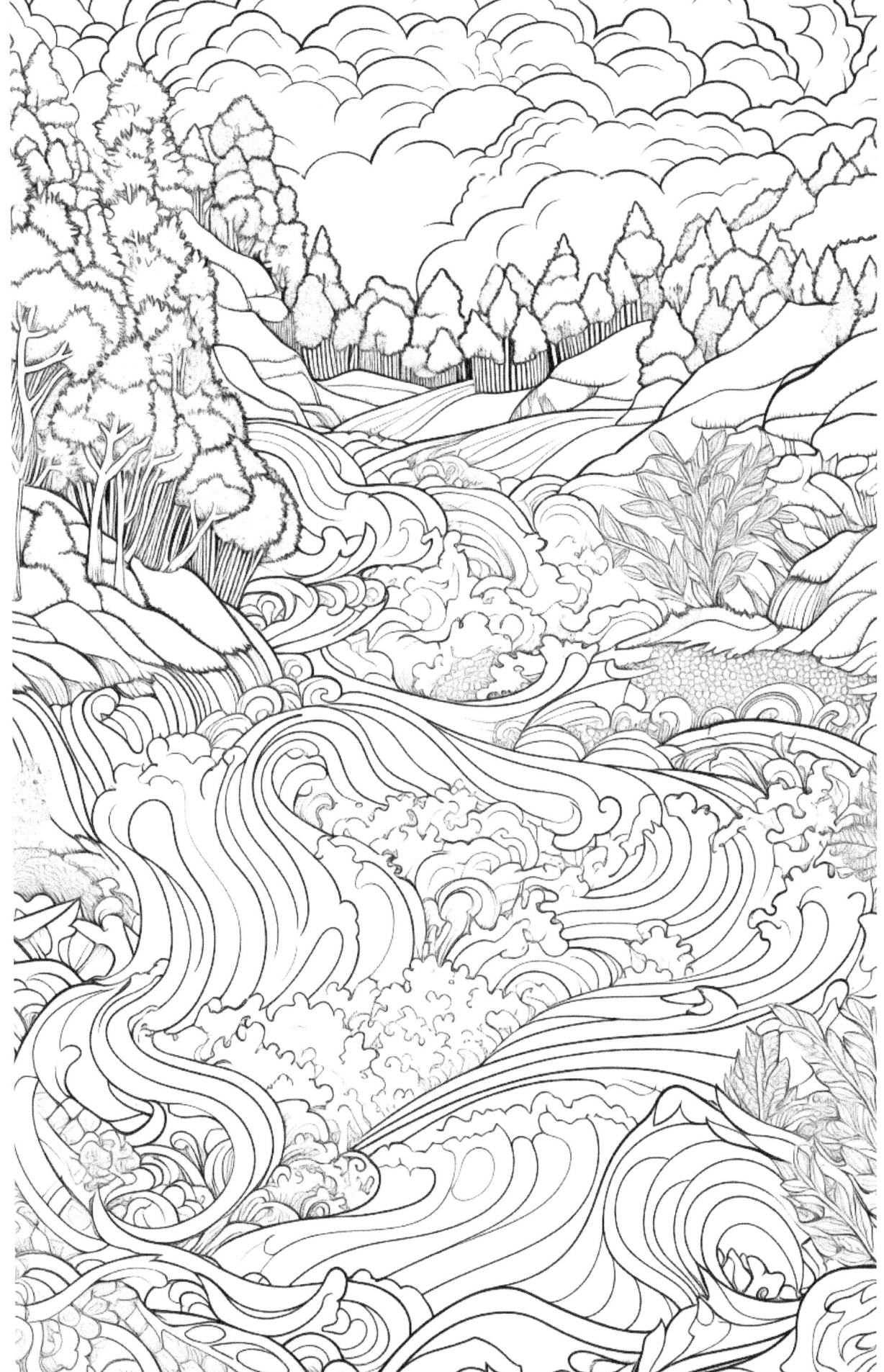

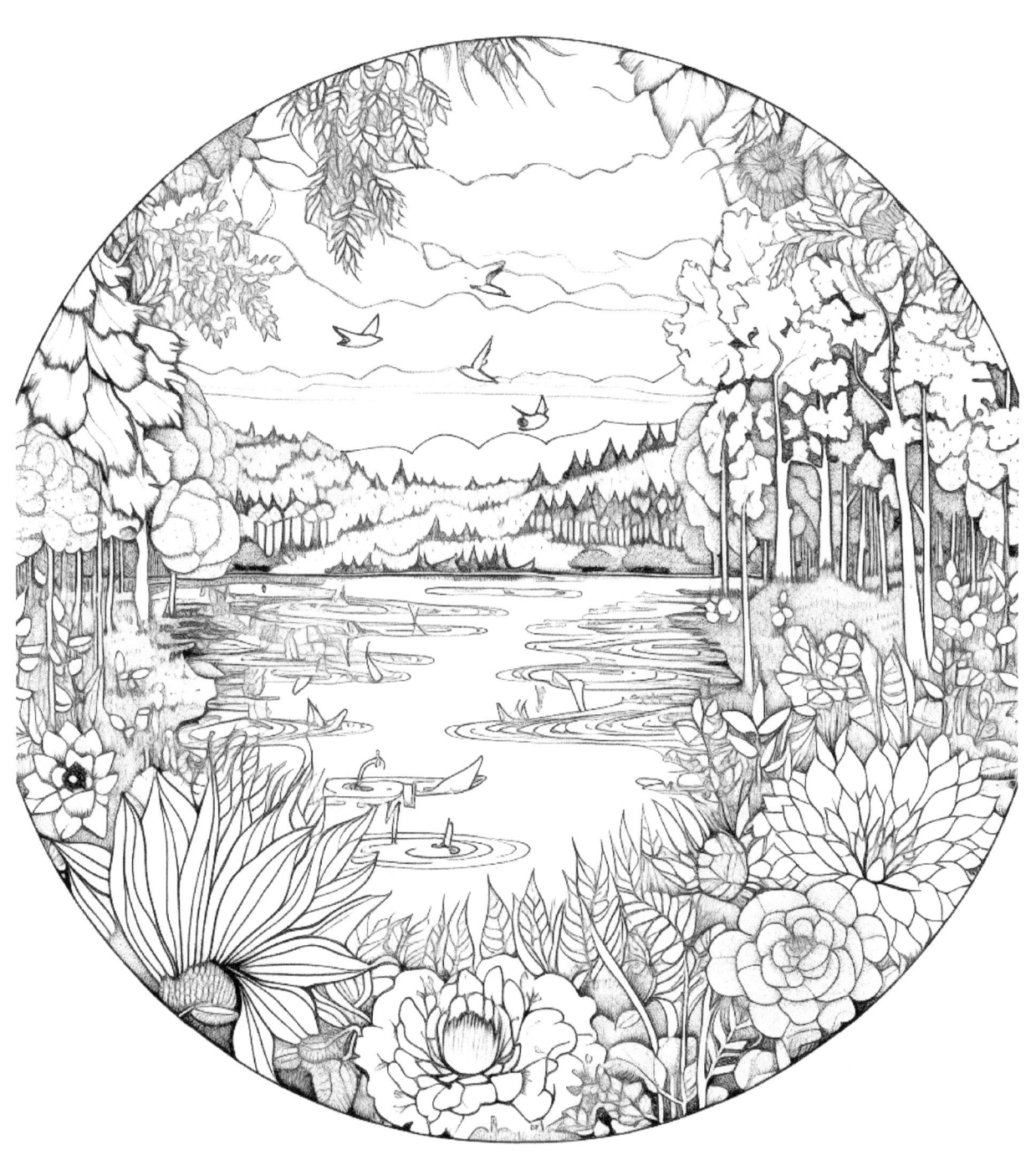

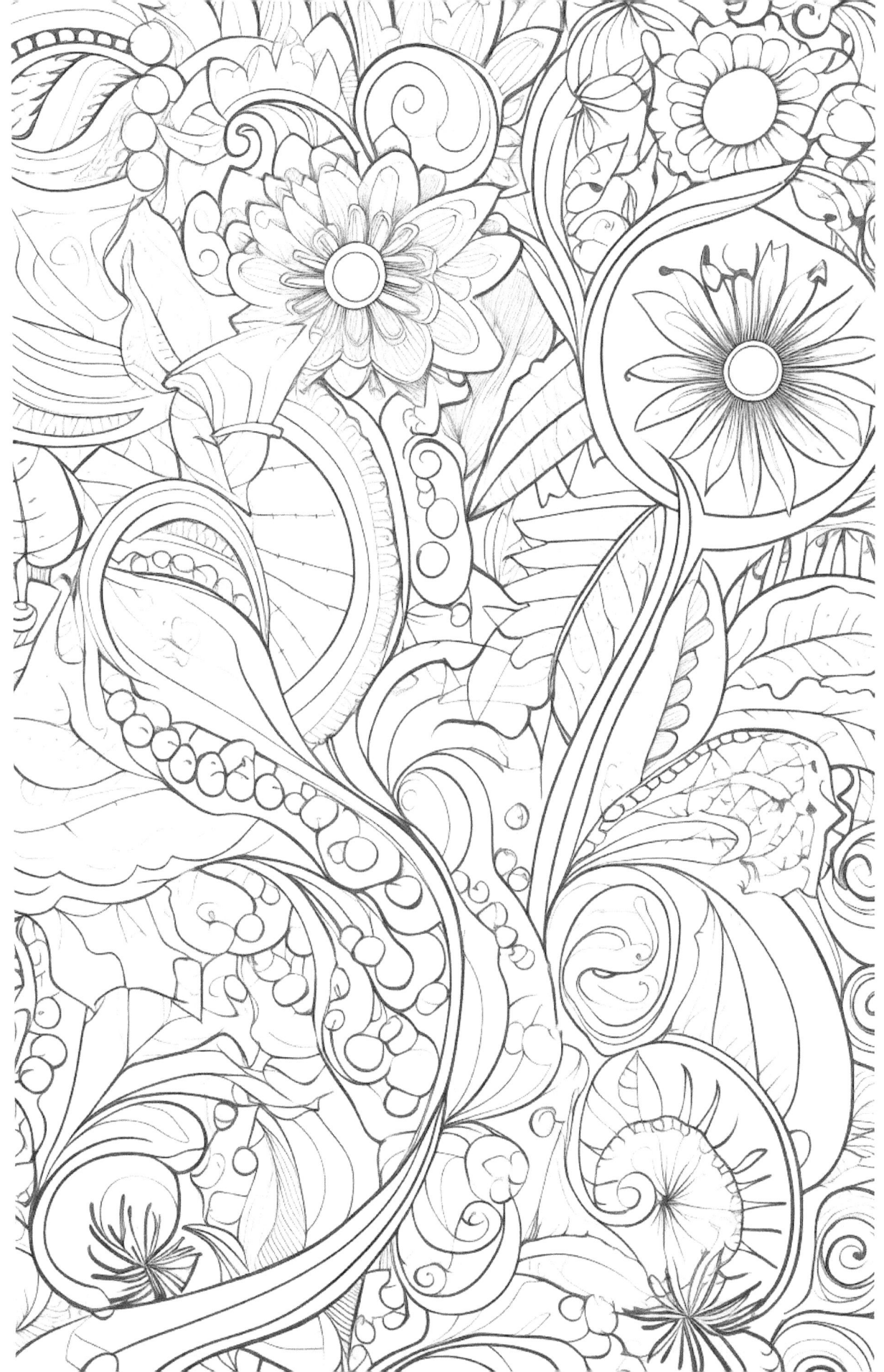

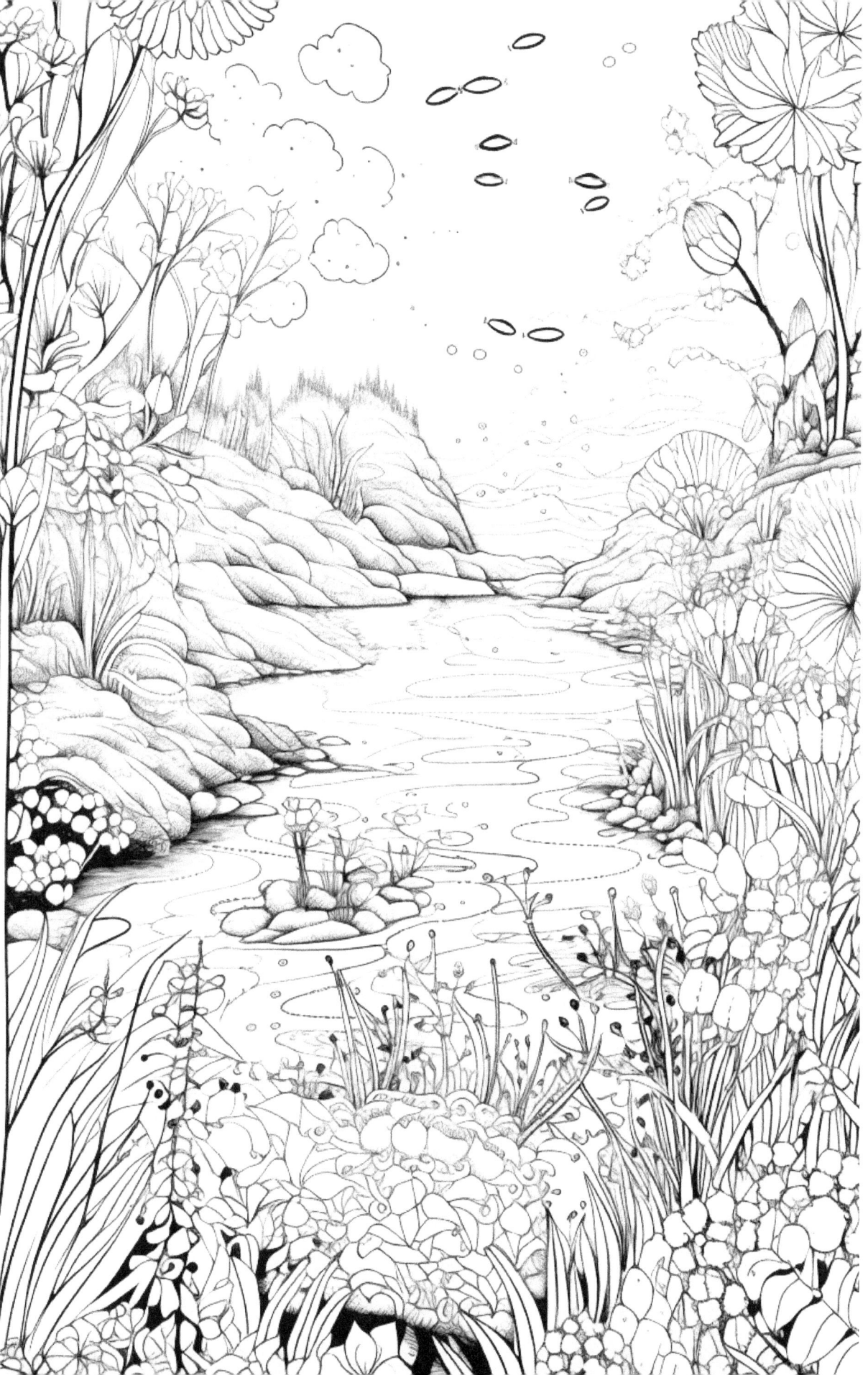